The Places Where There Are Spaces

Cultivating a Life of Creative Possibilities

Lisa Hopkins

◆ FriesenPress

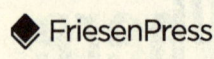

One Printers Way
Altona, MB R0G 0B0
Canada

www.friesenpress.com

Copyright © 2024 by Lisa Hopkins
First Edition — 2024

Podcast: STOPTIME:Live in the Moment
https://stoptimeliveinthemoment.buzzsprout.com/

All rights reserved.

No part of this publication may be reproduced in any form, or by any means, electronic or mechanical, including photocopying, recording, or any information browsing, storage, or retrieval system, without permission in writing from FriesenPress.

ISBN
978-1-03-830962-4 (Hardcover)
978-1-03-830961-7 (Paperback)
978-1-03-830963-1 (eBook)

1. BODY, MIND & SPIRIT, INSPIRATION & PERSONAL GROWTH

Distributed to the trade by The Ingram Book Company

For Mom
who taught me what it
means to dance.

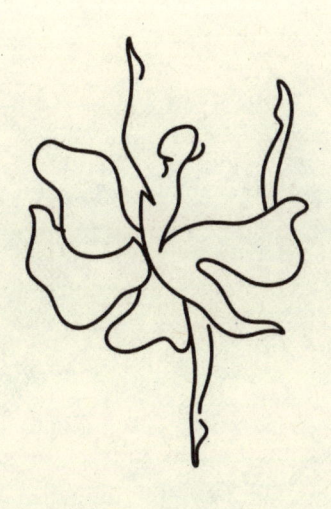

Contents

Preface	xi
1. This Too Shall Pass	1
2. The Power of IF	5
3. Getting to Know Your Inner Critic	9
4. What's Your Guiding Word?	13
5. Beyond Manifestation	16
6. The Milestone Myth	22
7. Navigating Your Own Course	27
8. Redefining Courage	30
9. Hitchhiking for New Rules of Thumb	33
10. Replacing FOMO with Curiosity	36
11. From Treading Water to Diving Deep	40
12. Limitless Beliefs	45
13. Use Your Words!	49
14. That Inescapable Fall Feeling	53
15. Wide-Awake Dreaming	56
16. The Fear of Abundance	59
17. The Many Shades of You	63
18. Pivot!	67
19. Learning How to Receive	70
20. The Syncopated Rhythm of Life	74

21. The Lies We Tell Ourselves	79
22. Carving Out Fresh Paths	82
23. Every Day I Make My Bed	86
24. Unpacking What Weighs Us Down	88
25. Say What You Need to Say	91
26. Our Limitless Capacity to Thrive	94
27. Every Day Is Your Birthday	98
28. Pages Left Unturned	102
29. The Power of Soup	107
30. The Wisdom of Wordle	110
31. Lessons from a Snake	114
32. Taking the Pressure off Flow	118
33. What Are You Tolerating?	122
34. First Thoughts and Overwhelm	126
35. The Call from Your Inner Agent	130
36. What Do You Want to Be When You Grow Up?	134
37. Portals to Possibilities	139
38. How Stepping Away from Your Work Makes You More Productive	145
39. How Did You Get Here?	149
40. Sorting Your Thought Garbage	152
41. The Journey Is the Thing	156
42. The Gifts in Grief	160
43. Lessons from the Lake	165

44. Reconnecting Lost Signals	168
45. The Magic of Letting Go	172
46. The Power of Energetic Choice	176
47. When Your Strength Becomes Your Weakness	180
48. Living Life as a Mosaic	185
49. Mental Blocks	188
50. The Art of Perspective	194
51. Little Impacts Everywhere	198
52. My Night at The Museum	201
53. The Paradox of Change	206
54. Life Is a Wide-Open Stage	209
55. When Your Networking Is Not Working	212
56. When Is Enough, Enough?	219
57. The Hurdles We Face in the Human Race	222
58. Holiday Hangovers	225
59. The Places Where There Are Spaces	229
I Am	232
Gratitude	233

"Between stimulus and response, there is a space. In that space lies our freedom and power to choose our response. In our response lies our growth and our freedom."

—Viktor Frankl, 1946

Living in the moment has always come naturally to me. Ever since I can remember, it's been second nature. I could always see the possibility in each moment, and even when moments were less than ideal, it was easy for me to find my light in the darkness, like glow-in-the-dark tape on the theatrical stage of life. For the longest time, I assumed that others were able to do the same, and when they couldn't, it frustrated me. It wasn't until I became a life coach that I discovered there was a way to share and express my gift of living in the moment in a more tangible way, beyond the proscenium.

In many ways, my lifelong career in the performing arts was all about the places where there are spaces. In theater, we begin with an empty space, and the way we position or "place" actors and scenery on the stage creates relationships and evokes meaning. In dance class, as in life, I was always drawn toward exploring and experiencing the spaces between the leaping and the landing, both as a student and as a teacher. My choreography was filled with space that allowed and invited perspective, energy, and breath.

This has been a long time coming; in fact, I'm pretty sure it's been inside of me all along. In any case it is literally a place where there was a space and I've chosen to be in the moment and fill it unconditionally and trusting the process as I share some concepts and ideas I've learned along the way.

This book is a collection of personal essays, self-inquiry, and musings that I have gathered in my journey—many of which were created or rewritten while staying in place in the Laurentian Mountains of Quebec during the global pandemic. Some are shared lessons, while others are more practical coaching exercises.

You will notice that I frequently refer to dictionary definitions. I make it a practice to delve deeper into words that I already know. In fact, the beginner's mindset has truly been a North Star for me, offering me the opportunity to explore and gain a deeper understanding of things.

Feel free to open the book and begin reading wherever you are drawn. I've included prompts after each chapter for you to consider along with places to respond, doodle, or jot down your insights. Be messy or neat, effusive or brief, or everything and anything in between, depending on how you are feeling. There is no right way to do it! You may be inclined to revisit your reflections after a time, to see if anything has shifted, or you may decide never to look at them again.

I hope that you enjoy this collection and that these chapters might provoke some insights or new ways of thinking that help you to connect to and reflect on what living in the moment means to you.

I am grateful to you for holding space for my words.

Lisa ♡

1. This Too Shall Pass

It had been almost six weeks since we left our Hell's Kitchen sublet in New York City. Broadway had shut down, the university had gone remote, and the world as we knew it had changed forever. It was a Friday night, although the days of the week were fast losing their meaning, as everything that used to be on our calendar had been canceled indefinitely. I knew it was Friday though, because it was time for Margarita Sunset, the festive ritual that I shared with my husband, who was the only human being I had seen in person since we fled from New York City.

I'm not sure why we chose margaritas instead of hot toddies on what was still a very cold and snowy April in Northern Quebec. Maybe it was a kind of holding on, a remnant of our former life in the city when we used to celebrate the end of the week with happy-hour margaritas at our favorite Mexican bar. I can still recall how strange it felt the last time we were there. It was Friday the thirteenth of March 2020, the day after the first coronavirus-related activity restrictions were issued. It would be two and a half years before we returned to New York City.

At the chalet, outside on the deck, I nestled into my Adirondack chair, wrapped in a sleeping bag with my knees tucked up to my chin. I was awaiting the sunset over the mountains from my front-row seat. The silhouetted branches of the barren trees stretched their limbs to the sky like dancers as nature's pre-show was about to begin. Straight ahead, the gentle slopes of the Laurentian Mountains patiently waited. I had recently learned that they are one of the oldest mountain ranges on Earth. They were formed around one billion years ago. How interesting that the younger mountains grew softer with age.

Just then, a fast-moving cloud scudded by in my peripheral vision, drawing my eye away from the mountain. I delighted as its puffy white turned pink as cotton candy catching the light just right. The phrase *This too shall pass* came into my head, and, although aware of the old adage's ability to bring comfort during difficult times, I wondered what it meant to me in that moment.

When King Solomon thought he'd teach his humble servant a lesson by sending him on the hapless mission to find the magical ring capable of making a sad man happy and a happy man sad, he never imagined that the servant would succeed. The king was astounded when his servant returned with the ring. Plain and unembellished, the ring was simply engraved with the words "This too shall pass." I thought more about the fable that is so often associated with the message that

The Places Where There Are Spaces

fortune means nothing in the end. Although there is great wisdom in that, I felt moved to dig in deeper.

When situations are bad, we just want them to be over, to get through and go back to the way it was when things were better. Or, at least in retrospect, they seemed better. Were they, though?

Anything seems better when we are suffering. When something negative happens, the only way we know that it is negative is in reference to something else. We rely on comparison to rate how we feel about our situations, our choices, and, most insidiously, how we rate ourselves. If the person who is unhappy with his life is comforted by "This too shall pass," what about the person who is happy with his life? Does this phrase make him sad?

I watched as the cloud continued its journey, drifting out of sight to reveal a clear sky. An overwhelming sense of joy and gratitude came over me as I thought about how wonderful these six weeks had been. I felt wistful for a moment as melancholy threatened to rise in me. *This too shall pass*, I thought.

Just then, my husband arrived with two margaritas in hand and sat down next to me. As we watched the sun setting over the mountains that Friday night, I vowed to savor every moment.

What might you be overlooking in the present by focusing on the past or the future?

2. The Power of IF

In the fall of 2015, we sublet a studio apartment on the first floor of a 76th Street brownstone on the Upper West Side. It was the very definition of boho, with its exposed brick and a sleep loft that we had to climb up and duck down to get into bed every night. The Museum of Natural History was just around the corner, and we often laughed and frolicked there after dark as we ran up and down the stone steps. We felt like newlyweds again—just the two of us alone together in the Big Apple, living like Bohemians as we had all those years ago when we first came to New York. Every morning, we woke to the lively sounds of the children playing outside in the schoolyard across the street. It was hard to believe that our baby had grown and flown and our first foray to NYC was a lifetime ago. Our sublet was for the fall semester, and like the college kids I was teaching downtown, we'd be heading home for the holidays in December.

I had just returned from a day of teaching and was putting the key in the door when I noticed it. The number on the door, which was once shiny gold with proud, bold black lettering, was now peeling away from the wood grain door, just above the peephole. I wondered about who put it there in the first place and whether they had recognized the irony—Apt #1F, which, to me, clearly spelled "IF."

The seemingly harmless, little two-letter word might be one of the most powerful in our vocabulary. It can serve as a master motivator, as it did for my students, propelling them toward their dreams, helping to fuel their passion despite all obstacles—"IF I work hard enough, I will reach my goals."

It also has the capacity to hold us back before we've had the chance to open ourselves up to possibility, especially when it's conditional: "I'll do it IF . . ."

Perhaps the most potent of all is when the word is wrapped up in regret, reminding us of missed opportunities or wishing we had acted differently: "IF only . . ."

We almost canceled our trip to NYC that fall. While dropping off our daughter at college in California, I got the call from my doctor in Vermont, diagnosing me with breast cancer. They advised me to come home for treatment, which was the opposite of what we had planned to do.

Never have I ever been further from living in the moment than when they gave me the diagnosis. Although it stopped me in my tracks, and required me to receive what I was hearing, it catapulted me into catastrophic-future thinking. I envisioned a future of chemo and radiation and felt myself slipping further and further away from my artist's life, allowing myself to be defined by my disease. But then I asked myself, *What IF?*

The Places Where There Are Spaces

What if there was another way? Instead of accepting that there was only one way to do things, I got curious and tapped into other possibilities. "What if?" became a powerful mantra for me during that difficult time and it empowered me to be my own advocate and to keep asking questions.

I smiled when I saw the moniker on my apartment door that day and felt glad that I had made the decision to come. It was a reminder of the endless array of possibilities that are open to us IF we open our minds and hearts and, indeed, our eyes to see them.

Think of a specific area of your life where "if" might serve as a beacon of new possibilities. What opportunities does it invite? What's one thing you can do today to apply this new insight?

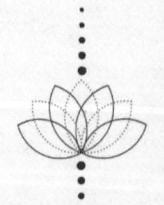

3. Getting to Know Your Inner Critic

Imagine a scenario in which you are the landlord and you have a tenant who has been living upstairs for as long as you can remember. The tenant is loud and opinionated and has, on many occasions, kept you up at night, no matter how hard you try to block out the noise. You've considered evicting them but do nothing instead, preferring to put up with it or try to ignore their remarks and avoid confrontation. And so, things stay the same even though the tenant doesn't contribute at all to your quality of life and criticizes you anytime you try to make any improvements. They don't even pay rent! In fact, it costs *you* to have them reside with you. And yet you let them stay. Now you might be thinking: *I would never put up with that!* And yet we do!

Imagine that upstairs is your head and the tenant is your inner critic. In coaching, we call it our "gremlin"—that little voice in your head that holds you back by telling you that you aren't good enough, aren't ready yet, or don't deserve success. We all have them. Gremlins take great pride in their role and think they know what's best for us. The more you try to resist them, the louder they will get. Despite what it feels like, they aren't nefarious creatures, there to take you down. They think they are keeping you safe. It's not much more than a big misunderstanding.

If you don't let them know that they aren't helping, they'll assume it's business as usual and keep creating feelings of inadequacy to keep you from embarrassing yourself or failing. They will stay "upstairs" in your head until you acknowledge them for what they are and invite them "downstairs," closer to your heart.

Once identified, it's natural to first feel anger and blame toward your gremlins and spend your days trying to evict them; however, as counterintuitive as it may seem, I encourage you to look at it differently. Gremlins are there for a purpose. They've been with you since you were born—they are a part of you.

When you recognize how much your gremlin has been blocking your path to success, invite them down and let them know that you understand the negative talk was intended to protect you. Validate them for wanting to help and acknowledge that it may very well have helped before, but you've got this now and don't need protecting. Maybe even offer them your thanks. This is where energy begins to be released and the foundation for a healthier relationship with your tenant begins. Instead of trying to lock them up or evict them, you can create a new role for them, one that will help you achieve your goals. Rewrite your gremlin's script with something that serves you. You don't need them to move out; they just need to understand that

The Places Where There Are Spaces

they'll be better able to help you move forward in their new role. Believe it or not, our gremlins want to know how they can help, and it's up to us to educate them on how.

Now imagine the next day, on your way to that audition or job interview, your tenant yells down to you: "You've got this!" And when you get home that night, instead of hearing all the reasons you may have screwed up that day, they tell you: "You did a great job today." And you smile, because you know in your heart that they are right.

Reflect on an outdated message that no longer serves you. Take a moment to rewrite this message. What would the new, supportive version sound like?

4. What's Your Guiding Word?

Never have so many of us felt so incredibly relieved to have a year behind us as we did when we said goodbye to 2020. I'm pretty sure most of us could easily come up with an infinite array of not-so-positive adjectives to describe the year that brought us a global pandemic.

Many people like to choose a word to guide them into the new year, a kind of intention setting or mantra. I *love* words, and yet I've never considered having one. So as 2020 was coming to an end, I went on a quest to find my guiding word for 2021.

At first, it was daunting because I was seeking for a word that was more than simply empowering; there are so many great ones. I yearned for a one bespoke to me—a word I could relate to that was magical and mysterious, a kind of talisman.

Then, as if by magic it came to me out of nowhere: caribou.

Caribou was the name of the place my husband and I were staying during year two of staying in place. Nestled on the edge of a snow-covered lake, surrounded by mountains, we had landed back home in the Great White North, far from the largest metropolis in the United States where we had spent most of our adult lives. It was some of the most beautiful nature I'd ever seen. A real city girl, I knew nothing about the gorgeous landscape that surrounded us, let alone the indigenous caribou.

To my delight, I discovered that besides being a magnificent animal, the caribou symbolizes a personal spiritual journey, and that the caribou are believed to be able to guide you to the spirit world and back—I was onto something. I could identify with the other words that I found to describe the noble caribou which included endurance, determination, adaptation, community, duality, and perseverance. Finally, and most surprising to me, was that unlike other species of deer, both male and female caribou have antlers. Gender equality—now that's my kind of animal! I had found it. My word for 2021 would be "caribou." I smiled, ready to embrace the spirit of this noble creature and let it guide me on my journey.

I have never enjoyed shoveling snow more than I had that year in Quebec, surrounded by the mountains. Every morning, I would go out on the frozen lake and make patterns and paths in the new fallen snow. The paths didn't lead anywhere in particular, but the shoveling brought me joy like I have never felt before. It turns out that the word "caribou" comes from the Mi'kmaq word which means snow shoveler. I have yet to encounter a caribou in my physical world; nevertheless, my spirit animal guided me wholeheartedly through 2021.

Reflect on a word that empowers and energizes you, serving as your guiding light into the next year or chapter of your life.

5. Beyond Manifestation

Imagine a charming French village nestled between vineyards and orchards, in the Eastern Townships of Quebec. An enchanted place, with a quaint auberge, a chocolatier, and Quebec's oldest twelve-sided barn. Tucked discreetly away off the main thoroughfare and aptly called Mystic, the French hamlet is just miles from the US border but worlds away from everything. Rarely noticed by outsiders, it seems to stand still in time, like a kind of French Canadian *Brigadoon*.

Now, in this magical place, imagine the pièce de résistance: a quintessential 1880 Anglican church that's been lovingly restored and converted to a unique residence. Can you imagine that? We did.

My husband discovered it on the realtor site, and the moment I saw it, I was captivated. Even though I was only looking at pictures, there was a kind of alchemy that transported me into each photograph. I walked through every room and looked out each window. I felt the long, cold winter thawing and saw the first buds of spring peeking out the window below the bell tower. I pictured us in the kitchen at wintertime, surrounded by family and friends, hosting holiday parties. In the summer, I imagined enjoying local wine and music events on the lawn. I could visualize the leaves changing color in the fall as the sun cast a beautiful golden light over our church and come harvest time, riding into wine country on our bikes and stomping the grapes at the fouloir. I envisioned it alright. One might even say I manifested it.

"Manifest" is a term thrown around so much these days. The *Oxford English Dictionary* defines it as "clear or obvious to the eye or mind." A manifest also refers to a list of cargo or passengers on a particular trip.

Did we manifest the vision of this mystical property all the way to our accepted offer and scheduled move-in date? I don't know. What I do know is that the definition of manifest as a list of cargo or passengers on a particular trip is precisely what my husband and I were. It was as passengers on the journey that our greatest joy unfolded, and the destination, as glorious as it might have been, was rendered insignificant in the grander scheme of things.

The thrill of the get was palpable. We knew that there would be no counteroffer from the owner and that we had just one chance to win the bid. At the eleventh hour, our agent called and suggested we write something from the heart about how we felt about the property. She thought it might make the difference. Her suggestion was a true gift indeed, a welcomed reprieve from suppressing our true feelings behind our contrived poker faces of negotiation.

She was right; it did make the difference. Despite the higher offer on the table, the owners were moved by what we wrote and accepted our bid instead. We reveled and toasted to an exciting new chapter. There is nothing as glorious as basking in a win.

It wasn't long before our rhetoric started to set in, and it sounded a lot like us trying to convince ourselves we had done the right thing. As the reality of what was to follow started seeping in (financing, inspections, paperwork, deadlines), so did the doubt. Romance and red tape don't make great dance partners, and what began as a romantic vision was now being threatened by worry and second thoughts.

The proverbial dance floor was getting crowded now and everybody was stepping on everyone's toes. The music, which was once so beautiful, had become overpowered by a cacophony of noise. It felt like we had to yell to be heard.

It was at that moment that the alchemy began, and things started to move in a new direction. Somehow, from that place, which could have so easily derailed us, we found ourselves moving away from feeling trapped by black-and-white thinking and toward recognizing and exploring what we were learning from this experience that we might not otherwise have known.

What followed was a different kind of dance with steps that, although unfamiliar, was slower and more deliberate and had a certain kind of synchronicity that we hadn't experienced together before. The pulse of the unexpected rhythm, although initially driven by fear, somehow converted into some of the most meaningful and honest interactions my husband and I have ever shared.

Instead of clinging to the shoulds and shouldn'ts that were so very clearly presenting themselves—we have committed, so we should just follow through, we shouldn't have gone this far if we weren't sure—or trying to convince ourselves that everything would be fine—we'll make it work, it'll be great—we took the time to listen. The kind of deep listening associated with being unattached to what we wanted to hear. The kind of listening inherent in unconditional love.

We took turns leading, and acknowledged and validated each other's thoughts and feelings, getting curious instead of defensive when we didn't see things the same way. We uncovered common ground that became the fertile soil in which we were able to dig deeper into the values rooted in the choices we were making together. We began paying attention to what we were heading toward, rather than what we were running from. When we stopped spending our energy on trying to find a loophole so we could renege on the offer, our rhythm became more fluid and in sync.

Suddenly all the possibilities were flowing back in reigniting our excitement about why we were inspired to buy the property in the first place. What had felt like obstacles were coming more easily now as we moved forward toward our vision. We remarked on how the experience had brought us closer together and how grateful we were to feel seen and heard by one another. In just one month, we'd be starting our new life in the mystical hamlet—on that charming country lane in the magical church that we had manifested!

Then we received an email. The property had tested positive for radon. It was our one contingency. We had an out. Even though we had managed to convince ourselves to move forward, legally, we could call it a deal-breaker and walk away. The owners promised to remediate the problem and the broker assured us that it would be easily resolved. The decision was ours. I looked at my husband and felt more connected to him than ever before. He looked back at me and smiled. We knew in that moment that we'd be more than okay no matter what we decided, and so, with unconditional love, we agreed wholeheartedly to retract our offer.

Whether or not we manifested all of this, I will never know. But what I do know for certain is that you can't put a price on what we learned that day and the return on investment from the experience itself is what holds the greatest value. And that is nonnegotiable.

What would you do differently if—no matter what decision you made—you couldn't fail?

6. The Milestone Myth

Whether or not you ever dreamed of college or know someone that does, the limiting beliefs around what going to college represents are so ubiquitous that you can't help but feel the weight of their impact on so many kids—and their parents.

As a college professor and a parent, I am well acquainted with the construct and the power we ascribe to this so-called monumental rite of passage. It's not the only place in our lives that we create milestones for ourselves without considering why we even wanted to go there in the first place—or what we'll do when we finally get there (insert: more money, better job, bigger house, smaller pant size). So, on this first day of May, I find myself thinking about what might be learned from all of this and invite you to follow along with this little story I created to help us explore.

Meg says she wants to go to college but is failing her classes in her junior year. Her mom is beside herself with worry and frustration. She just can't understand why her daughter doesn't put any effort into getting her assignments in on time. It's not that she isn't bright or couldn't pass—if only she would just put her mind to it. Meg's actions just don't seem to match what she says she wants to do. There's a disconnect, a paradox that's affecting her chances of getting into college, and it's creating a rift between Meg and her mom.

Mom has a fixed mindset around what wanting to go to college looks like, and she's got plenty of hard data to support her point of view. She's at the ready with tools and strategies to help Meg get there and has tried everything from wall calendars and Post-it note systems to pulling all-nighters helping with homework, but nothing seems to work. Meg is as disengaged as ever, and Mom is exhausted from pushing so hard.

From Meg's perspective, it's been made crystal clear what she is supposed to do and equally evident that she is not behaving as prescribed by literally everyone around her, from her college counselor to her well-meaning grandparents and friends. Overwhelmed by expectations and being told what she should do, Meg feels out of control. Disconnected. The one thing she can control, though, is NOT doing what she's supposed to do.

Mom thinks Meg wants to go to college for all the wrong reasons and that she only wants to be a doctor because she watches *Grey's Anatomy*. Concerned that her daughter doesn't see the reality of the situation, Mom bears down on her efforts to help Meg pass her courses and save her from certain embarrassment when all her friends are posting their acceptances on social media.

The instinct to protect our children comes so naturally that it feels like it's the right thing to do. It fuels our power to persist, even though the harder we push, the more they pull away. Unfortunately, while the mom in this story was so busy focusing on the hard data of the *how to's*, she was missing some vital clues to be discovered in the soft data in her daughter's *whys*.

Meg is certainly not the first to envision herself in med school like the characters on *Grey's Anatomy* or to dream of the college experience, so seductively curated by the college board. It's the obvious next step, already mapped out, almost expected. I am reminded of a glossy college brochure I once saw with a photo of the perfectly manicured campus and an arrow with a label that said, "Insert yourself here."

I binge-watched *Grey's Anatomy* as a middle-aged woman ten years after it had aired. Not once did I look back at my life and think that I would have liked to have been a doctor. What I related to most about the show was the metaphor drawn between life and the practice of medicine. It makes me wonder what the daughter in this story is really being pulled toward and if she's ever asked herself that question?

It's much easier to choose the prepackaged all-inclusive experience that tells you what you want rather than doing the deeper/harder work of uncovering your values and creating your own way. No wonder so many kids arrive on the campus of their dreams only to find that it isn't all that it promised to be. Blaming themselves, believing it must be them that doesn't fit, that they don't measure up.

We all identify with things for different reasons. There's no one-size-fits-all value system. We may both choose to do the same thing but our reasons for doing it are what makes our experience unique, what makes us feel connected to our choices. Whether or not Meg passes her senior year and goes to college in this story is not important. What matters is that whatever she decides derives from a deeper, more meaningful place than a milestone, a college campus, or a career. A place that is aligned with values that she can honor, wherever she goes. A lesson that you can't be taught at school.

What core values are connected to the goals that you have set for yourself?

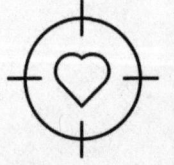

7. Navigating Your Own Course

Have you ever shared a thought or an idea before you've had a chance to process it yourself? Testing the waters, you float the idea to friends or family, hoping they'll get on board. If they don't, do you second-guess yourself, wondering if you were just being silly or selfish for even thinking it in the first place? And then, based on the new insecure thoughts that are flooding your brain about the original idea, you decide not to rock the boat, convincing yourself that it is better to suppress your thoughts than to make any waves. So, you bottle it up and toss it away into the sea of unprocessed ideas and move on with the more predictable, familiar terrain of life as you know it.

Alternatively, what happens if they *do* get on board with your idea right away? A sudden current of affirmation washes over you, and, buoyed by their support, you ride the wave of enthusiasm, eager to impress. The course has been clearly mapped out for you, charted by the opinions of well-meaning friends and family. And so, you show up as expected, arriving at all the scheduled ports of call on time. Remember that little idea that you once felt *drawn toward*? It has now grown into something you are being *pushed into*, without giving yourself the chance to consider why.

The need for external validation is real; it can even propel us toward doing things we hadn't imagined we could do. And it's perfectly natural to want to feel championed by those we love, a quick energy boost. But at the end of the day, road, or journey, there's only you. *They* aren't connected to the thing *you* wanted to do; they've tied it to what matters to *them*. So, when you arrive at the destination—the one where you thought you wanted to go—you feel like a castaway stranded on a desert island, trying to remember why you even wanted to go there in the first place. Where is everyone? They've moved on. They're good!

However well-meaning your friends and family are, they don't know what is best for you. Only you know what is best for you. The rush we feel from external validation is nothing more than a quick hit. It's unsustainable. What will keep us on course is truly connecting to why things really matter to us.

So, the next time you have a new idea, take the time you need to process it *before* you spill it out or bottle it up. Your thoughts are there for a reason, and when you take the time to explore what they signify, you can take the helm and navigate your own course.

What's something you'd like to do no matter what anyone thinks?

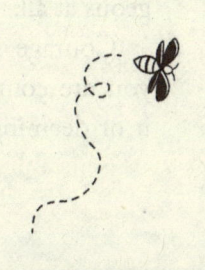

8. Redefining Courage

Shame researcher Brené Brown contends that vulnerability is our most accurate measure of courage and poses the question: "Are we willing to show up and be seen when we can't control the outcome?" The question I've been asking is: "Are we willing to *not* be seen when we are courageous?"

The definition of courage has been spoon-fed to us since we were children. As parents, we have become avid encouragers, making it abundantly clear how high a value society places on courage. We've been taught to know what it looks like, that's it's measurable, that it can be seen. The Merriam-Webster dictionary tells us that the word "encourage" suggests "the raising of one's confidence especially by an external agency." I am discovering, though, that internal agency is where our courage resides and that often the things that have demanded the most courage—the things seem Goliath to us—by others' standards wouldn't rank as courageous at all.

Courage is personal. And I'm willing to bet that you are courageous every day without even realizing it or deeming it worthy of recognition. If you are not

The Places Where There Are Spaces

recognized for your courage, were you even courageous at all?

It is the bravest thing you can do to confront the things within yourself without the need to share with others, and let it be enough that *you know* you were courageous. True courage is not dependent on any associated badge of honor or praise doled out by others with a "Good for you!" or the victorious declaration you make on your social media.

Often, the most courageous thing you can do is to believe in yourself. Courage is a spectrum: unique, personal, and as fluid as our experiences themselves.

Like anything worth mastering, courage takes practice. I encourage you to stretch and condition your inner knowing muscle so that you can appreciate and see how courageous you already are.

How do you define courage?

9. Hitchhiking for New Rules of Thumb

I have never hitchhiked in the literal sense, never stood on the side of a road and stuck my thumb out, hoping a passing vehicle would stop and pick me up. When I think of hitchhiking, it conjures up all sorts of familiar tropes and cautionary tales. The Merriam-Webster definition of hitchhike is "to be carried or transported by chance or unintentionally." I'm not so sure I agree with that description. I'll tell you why.

What stands out to me the most is the idea that, despite the inherent dangers, the hitchhiker has discerned that the fear of staying where they are is far greater than the fear of where they are going. Unattached to knowing where the journey will take them, they show up on the side of the road and extend their arm with a deliberate, emphatic, literal thumbs up to chance. That, from my point of view, qualifies as intention. The definition of hitchhike cited earlier is more aptly applied to the word "hijacked," as so many of us felt during the pandemic. None of us intended to be "carried or transported by chance" to where we are now. We were essentially hijacked, diverted from where we thought we were going to where we are today.

We've all experienced that "How did I get here?" feeling of time slipping past without us noticing. And we've all been guided in one way or another by principles or "rules of thumb" along the way. A rule of thumb is a generally accepted guideline or method of doing something based on common practice rather than evidence or facts. A simple example is the convention of not wearing white after Labor Day.

There were no guidelines or standards for what to do after a global pandemic and yet as we moved toward reopening, we found ourselves standing at a crossroads that, if we were willing, offered us the opportunity to create new rules of thumb for ourselves, to chart new maps, and travel new pathways both neural and rural.

We mustn't rely on massive disruptions like a global pandemic to be the catalyst for change. Take inventory now of what is and what isn't working. The road is shorter than we imagine, and the final destination is the same for all of us.

Like the hitchhiker, we have the chance to choose old rules of thumb and return to life as we knew it, or we can ask ourselves whether the fear of staying where we are is greater than the fear of where we might go.

In what areas of your life are you following old standards instead of forging new paths?

10. Replacing FOMO with Curiosity

We've all felt FOMO, the fear of missing out, that nagging, anxiety-producing sense that something better or more interesting is happening somewhere else, without us. The feeling is real and utterly human. And, if we are being honest, something we've all felt more often than we'd care to admit.

I like to think of FOMO as the evil sibling of curiosity.

The benefits of curiosity are well-documented. Defined by *Cambridge Dictionary* as "an eager desire to know or learn something," curiosity helps us become better problem-solvers, overcome our fears, and develop empathy and connection.

FOMO, on the other hand, has no redeeming qualities—it isn't pretty. It's fast-moving, narrowly focused, and ego-centered and often masquerades as interest and feigns curiosity. When we're leading from FOMO, we aren't displaying any genuine interest at all, beyond how it might affect us. It can make us feel bad about ourselves and resentful toward others. *I never get those chances; Good things never happen to me.*

The Places Where There Are Spaces

It's characterized by a lack mentality that fosters and fuels greed, making it difficult to appreciate what we've already got. It reeks of entitlement: *Maybe I should do that, get that, have that.*

At the heart of FOMO is comparison, and in our curated world of people living their best lives on social media, it's no wonder it is so ubiquitous. Thoughts like *I need, I want* are suddenly at the forefront—often about something you never even thought about doing or having in the first place!

FOMO doesn't only occur when you are home alone wishing you were somewhere else. I have encountered it in alarming frequency in ordinary conversations; for instance, when one friend tells the other about a new gadget they have, and the other friend responds by taking out their phone—instead of taking any interest—to see if they can order one for themselves on Amazon. *Maybe I should do that, have one of those!* Bulldozing any chance for connection.

I'll be honest: when I'm in the presence of someone leading from FOMO, it elicits a feeling in me and associated thoughts that I'm not proud of having. Not only has my intention to share been thwarted, but I become angry and resentful at feeling angry and resentful!

It takes two people to share, to learn, to connect. When there are two people and none of these inherent possibilities are touched upon, it's like a one-sided tennis game where the ball is served and you keep it for your own, ending the possibility of play or engagement.

A new acronym in the English lexicon has emerged: JOMO, the joy of missing out. It describes the pleasure of taking a break from social activity—especially social media—to enjoy personal time. I like the sentiment and understand the value of stepping away from comparison, but it strikes me that there is a higher value at stake here that is being overlooked, which is not so black and white as simply walking away and renaming it. Why not learn from your "FOMatic" urges and explore the reasons why you feel compelled to compare? Become curious about your own behavior rather than jealous of others and use that moment as an opportunity to grow. If FOMO is fast-moving, narrowly focused, and ego-centered, then why not slow down, widen your lens, and not make everything about you?

How would your experiences change if you released the grip of FOMO and redirected your energy toward the thrill of engagement?

11. From Treading Water to Diving Deep

A couple of years ago, I was having lunch with a friend with whom I had collaborated closely in various artistic capacities throughout my career. He was the first person outside of my family who I "came out to" as a coach. When I proudly announced that I had completed my training and was now practicing as a certified life coach, he was unfazed. It was as if I had asked him to pass me the salt. He simply looked back at me and replied, "You mean get paid for what you've been doing your whole life?"

I made a significant commitment to my coach training. I dedicated eighteen months and over three hundred training hours to the most comprehensive accredited coach training program available. I was the only performing arts professional in a cohort of highly successful individuals, including physicians, entrepreneurs, and CEOs. I tried my very best not to draw attention to this fact, fearing that it would define me among my distinguished colleagues. I didn't want to be perceived as a novelty, an anomaly, or worst of all a shiny object.

The Places Where There Are Spaces

On the third day of training, word got out, and the lead trainer invited me to lead the class in a midday dance break. *Here we go again*, I thought to myself as I reluctantly took the stage. Although I couldn't deny how the mood of the room was transformed when I led the class, my colleague was surprised when he later asked me if it had been the highlight of my day, and I shared that it was quite the opposite.

I grappled with the limiting belief that my performing arts background diminished my credibility as a coach. Even more triggering was the perspective of my peers. Now that they knew about my background, they encouraged me to leverage my performing arts network to build my coaching practice. This sounded disingenuous to me, and so instead, I did the very opposite and I separated my two worlds.

I immersed myself in the study and practice of coaching and although intense, I felt invigorated by it. It was no problem to dance all day and then hit the books into the wee hours of the night. I was growing!

I managed to silo my two worlds, which allowed me the unique opportunity to reflect on my life as an artist through my new lens as a coach. I came to realize that while I still loved my performing arts career, my relationship to it had changed. The coach training allowed me to build upon and stretch the skillset I already had, and it also shone light on the muscles that had grown strong in my other career by keeping me in one place. What got me there was not what is going to get me to where I want to go next.

I thought again about my dance career and wondered when I had stopped swimming and become a water-treader. It was hard to pinpoint. Effortless and comfortable, it didn't feel like I was working hard to stay afloat; in fact, my treading felt more like stopping to admire the sunset or to smell the proverbial roses—it almost felt like mindfulness. I took pride in my ability to recognize and enjoy where I was at that moment. It was one of my gifts.

The American Red Cross includes treading water for one minute as part of their water competency skills. It's a valuable lifesaving skill—if you are actually stranded in deep waters. It takes strength and a great deal of energy to stay in one place for any length of time.

Without realizing it, over the years, I had become very good at remaining in the same place in my career. Although anyone who knew me would attest to my capabilities and enthusiasm for what I was doing, the danger lay in what psychologist Susan David, in her book *Emotional Agility*, refers to as being too competent. She says, "When we get too good at something, we can quickly find ourselves lulled back into autopilot mode, reinforcing not just rigid behavior but also disengagement, lack of growth, and boredom—in short, we fail to thrive."

Although I never felt bored with what I was doing, the autopilot mode was real. It was easy for me, and I loved what I was doing which is what made it hard to discern.

The Places Where There Are Spaces

My inclination to keep my coach training separate and my reluctance to come out as a coach in my artistic community, or as a dancer in my coaching realm, were based on the limiting belief that I couldn't be both—that they were mutually exclusive. I believed that any change of direction would dilute my commitment to my art or signify a change of heart, a departure from who I had always been.

I realize now that not only is it possible to be both, but, at least for me, it is imperative. They're both integral parts of who I am, and they are fluid. There is an ebb and flow that is contextualized, and the possibilities flood in when I let go of how they are supposed to look. Once I recognized that I was expending a whole lot of energy doing the same thing the same way, I was able to dive deeper and create some space for perspective and new ways of thinking. This allowed me to see that each enriches and supports the other. They integrate seamlessly.

Those water-treading skills still come in handy at times, especially when waters get rough, but now I use them intentionally as needed, not by default, because it's what I'm used to.

Oh, and my friend at lunch that day? He was right. I have always been a coach, just as I have always been an artist.

Where in your career or relationships might you be staying in place without realizing it?

12. Limitless Beliefs

We live in a world of metrics and standards. With more information available about everyone else's lives than we can handle, it's easy to judge and compare ourselves, to subscribe to the belief that we can never measure up. Feeling this way is as torturous as it is ubiquitous. We run ourselves ragged on the treadmill of life, work, and relationships, trying to prove our worth, hoping to bust through and finally arrive—to be enough. "No pain, no gain" might have been a mantra that helped you go the extra mile at some stage of your life, like when you were first developing your skills as a kid, a student, or earlier in your career. How many of us pulled up our legwarmers to dance to the tune of Debbie Allen's words in the movie *Fame*: "You want fame? Well fame costs, and right here is where you start paying—in sweat."

Although this kind of thinking may have served us once, it is highly possible that it has since become a limiting belief, a default way to inspire or motivate ourselves that just doesn't seem to be working anymore. No shaming here; we all have had ideas and beliefs that we've adopted along the way that we never questioned because they helped us get somewhere, protected us from something, or maybe just hadn't been proven otherwise. I mean, there was a time where we all accepted that the world was flat.

If I just push a little harder, I'll achieve even more, you tell yourself, believing that's what will take you to the next level. And so, you do push harder, achieve more, and still feel that you are never enough. Sound familiar? Why does it feel like it's all pain and no gain now?

It's time to call out our limiting beliefs and create some new limitless beliefs about ourselves that better serve who we are today.

Let's break it down a bit.

Ask yourself where this message of falling short is coming from. It's easy enough to blame the industry, the media, the world we live in, or even others for making you feel this way; however, once you own up to the fact that the message is coming from inside of you, we can begin dismantling its destructive, counterproductive effects.

Being cognizant of our abilities comes with an inherited duty to fulfill our potential and use our gifts to make an impact during our limited time here on the planet. And so, we drive ourselves forward to be better, work harder to be more of who we know we can be. The awareness of our gifts is a gift itself, but it is here that we need to make the distinction between living up to our potential and being enough—the distinction between obligation and responsibility.

While obligation has the potential to get us to do things, it is limited and disconnected from our values or reasons that we do things—our why. It differs, however, from a responsibility, which is defined in the *Oxford English Dictionary* as "the opportunity or ability to act independently and make decisions without authorization." When you are response-able, you take back your power to create the limitless life you want to lead.

The opposite of obligation? *Freedom.*

I believe that we always do the very best we can in any given moment, that nobody plays to lose. But it's important to remember that just as no two moments are ever the same, our best does not always look the same. So why then do we judge ourselves out of context?

Self-judgement takes up energetic space. It pulls focus from what we want to do and distracts us from accessing the energy we need to perform, excel, or deliver and show up as our best. Our energy is drained by these unproductive notions and comparisons when we need it most!

We are not machines. There are many things that affect our ability to achieve our highest potential in any given moment. These influencers are internal and external and, if we get curious and examine them, will provide clues for how to adjust course or set ourselves up for success in different situations. At the end of the day though, it's up to us; it's our response-ability to transform those limiting beliefs into beliefs that are unlimited.

Explore any limiting beliefs you may have about your abilities or worth. How do these beliefs influence your actions? Are they rooted in obligation or responsibility?

∞

13. Use Your Words!

Why don't we take more care with the words we use? Are we really in such a hurry that we'd rather speak quickly than take the time to say what we really mean to say?

I recently binge-watched *Downton Abbey* and found myself mesmerized by the characters' keen articulation and expression of the English language. From the scullery maid, all the way up to the upper echelon of high society, their vocabulary was vivid and rich. Although there was a clear class distinction in their accents, denizens of both upstairs and downstairs were equally comfortable and deliberate with the words they chose to speak. Granted, it's a scripted television series, but nonetheless, it got me thinking.

What would be different if we dug deeper into our lexicon and discovered words that aligned more closely with what we were really trying to say, rather than grabbing the first one that comes to mind? What if we didn't engage in using meaningless fillers— the uhms and ahs that save us from the uncomfortable awkward pauses or, worse yet, act like a kind of filibuster and discouraging discourse and any chance of connection? And why does the art of speaking refer only to public speaking? What about the art of speaking in everyday communication? In his book *The Four Agreements*, Don Miguel Ruiz tells us to be impeccable with our word—to speak with integrity, honesty, and truthfulness, and say only what we mean. But unless we choose our words carefully, how are we able to do that?

We tell our children to use their words when they are upset. Studies show that giving words to feelings (affect labeling) can make them become a lot less overwhelming or upsetting. Evidence shows that labeling our feelings is a form of emotion regulation. As children, our vocabulary was limited, and so we used more general words like "happy," "mad," or "sad." As adults, however, we have the ability—the opportunity—to articulate more clearly what we want to express. The word sad for example, may not mean the same to me as it does for you. A quick Google search for the synonym for "sad" offers us more than thirty-five choices, including "gloomy," "dejected," "regretful," and "downhearted."

There is a thrill in finding the perfect word to describe what we mean, but if we don't take the time to grow our vocabulary and practice using our new words, we won't be able to access them under stress. We will default to overused words, forgoing any chance of original thought. It isn't easy but, like anything worth developing, it takes courage and commitment.

Word shaming is real. Have you ever had someone you know call you out and tease you when you use a word that you haven't used before? I know I have.

The Places Where There Are Spaces

This kind of behavior discourages us from learning and scares us away from demonstrating new knowledge. I'm also willing to wager that very few of us haven't been heckled for mispronouncing a word or maybe even come across a word that they've been saying incorrectly their whole life. Some words are misused so often that their original meaning has changed over time. "Awful," for example, originally meant full of wonder, and "terrific" meant to evoke fear. Now, after time, they've been used incorrectly so often that they depict the exact opposite.

The good news is we have bountiful resources at our fingertips—should we decide to use them. There really is no excuse for not using our words powerfully. There is an endless array to choose from and we all have an opportunity to use our words intentionally and become our own thought leaders.

It occurs to me that words aren't dissimilar from values in that you can either pay lip service to them or you can be fully connected to their meaning and why you chose them. And, like each one of us, words have origin stories! How cool is that?

Consider specific situations where being clearer with your words might enhance your message and foster better communication.

14. That Inescapable Fall Feeling

There's an inescapable feeling that fall brings. It elicits a physical response in the pit of my stomach and an impulse to both hide and explore at the same time. The angle of the sun or the rustle of a tree branch against the cold blue sky can trigger it; at once lonely and ominous and, just as quickly, vibrant and full of opportunities to start something new. A beginning and an ending—all at the same time.

As children, fall brought that unique back-to-school feeling—a mix of fear and excitement for the new start of school and what possibilities lay ahead. New clothes, fresh books, and a schedule—all planned out for us. Isn't it funny that as adults we have such a binary relationship with schedules; on the one hand, we resent them and on the other, we desperately crave them. As kids, our fall schedule was more like a lottery, one that determined who our teacher would be and what kids were in our class. You never knew which teacher might change your life trajectory or if a classmate might become a lifelong friend. All we were required to do was show up.

There are lessons we can learn from how we rolled when we were children. We weren't worried about the big picture future (our parents and teachers did all that for us), and we were laser-focused on navigating the immediate future—the next class, the next glance from a bully or a crush. Each moment had a heightened significance that felt like it could be our last. We lived the highs and lows as they came before we learned how to bottle them up inside or became trained to manage our emotions. In many ways, we were truly living in the present and feeling all the feels that each moment of everyday brought. Unaware that we were doing it, we were choosing courage and vulnerability over fear of the unknown. We were masters of living in the moment.

And so, as the long days of summer inevitably fade into the early fall sunset and that inescapable fall feeling comes over you, don your favorite boots and sweater, breathe in the crisp fall air, linger in a bookstore, and enjoy the fruits of the harvest.

Let it be a reminder to slow down, embrace your inner child, and live in the moment. It's an invitation to let go of longing for the past and to schedule some time for yourself to *not* worry about the future *today*.

What's one thing that you can put on your schedule that is just for you?

15. Wide-Awake Dreaming

Sometimes, my best ideas surface when I wake up in the middle of the night. It's a kind of twilight zone when my inner critic is still dormant, unable to comment or judge, and my creative brain is clear and flowing freely—wide-awake dreaming.

When this happens, instead of falling back asleep, I get up, as I did earlier this week at 3:30 a.m. Like a mouse tiptoeing past a sleeping cat, I slipped out of bed into the other room, trying to stay in the zone. My creative brain knew that, if roused, hyper-vigilant brain would reprimand me for being up and try to scare me back to bed by telling me I was going to be too tired to function the next day. It would then use its amnesic alchemy and I'd forget the ideas, or worse yet remember them but somehow be convinced they were useless gibberish. Then the wrestling match would begin and the fear of being too tired would take over, ironically preventing me from going back to sleep again. The ticking clock would serve as a nagging reminder of how much time I was losing, and God forbid I'm still not sleeping when the birds start to wake up singing, "I-had-a-good-sleep-I-had-a-good-sleep," shaming me for not taking better care of myself.

The Places Where There Are Spaces

That night, I managed to stay in the zone long enough to jot down some ideas. They won't change the world or help me achieve anything; they are just words. Unattached to any kind of desire, solution, or outcome. No promises or particular purpose, just thoughts that became words on the page. My words. They came out of me.

Days later, when I first looked at the words through the lens of my physically awake self, they were fragmented and not particularly poignant. But they invited me to get to know them, assemble and disassemble them, like the child who plays with blocks, enjoying the building as much as the demolishing, happily crashing down creations to rebuild new ones. What you are reading now is some of what was generated. Although there was much more than what's on this page, the experience has provided me some food for thought and an opportunity to reflect. I should mention that I fell asleep easily that night after I captured some of the thoughts. Maybe I should do it more often.

Journal on what conditions make you feel most creatively inspired. (Consider place, time and physical & mental states)

16. The Fear of Abundance

The harvest has long been used as a metaphor for life. When we are patient and mindful, the old idiom "We reap what we sow" can truly be a guiding light, a harbinger for good things to grow. Sometimes, we sow seeds unknowingly. I read somewhere that dandelions have as many as four hundred seeds, which, when blown, can sail as far away as five miles!

Sowing seeds is the easy part, often accompanied by great enthusiasm and a vision of what they might become. I used to think the hardest part was seeing it through, staying true to the vision of what we've planted, cultivating an environment in which the seed can thrive and grow. Now, in my own moment of flourishing, I'm wondering if the reaping part might be the hardest thing of all. It really gets me thinking about our capacity to receive and accept good things when they come.

How many times have you heard someone say something hopeful and then quickly take it back for fear of jinxing it? Superstition tells us that speaking positively about our current situation may cast bad luck and invoke Murphy's Law, and that if anything can go wrong, it will. If fear were a muscle, we would be the weightlifting champions. But even the strongest weightlifters can develop muscle imbalances.

We are hardwired to protect ourselves from the things that we don't understand, to proceed with caution, and only go as fast as we can control or handle. It's no wonder we feel doubt or fear creep in when things seem to be going our way. Doubt and skepticism promise to keep us safe, but safe from what? There is no actual danger; these are primitive instincts for modern-day situations.

What might be different if we strengthened our muscles to receive, to reap the rewards without a caveat of fear? What if we were strong enough to accept our good fortune, the accolade, or the so-called "luck" as easily as we carry the weight and worry of expecting the worst? What if we were to carry our good fortune with gratitude as we move through life and accept it as part of what is, not explain it away as an anomaly or superstition?

Instead of waiting for the other shoe to drop, why not step into believing in yourself and realizing that it was *you* that created your abundance. You have worked for what you've earned. You've put in the time and cultivated the seeds. And like the dandelion whose seeds have scattered far and wide, who knows what other seeds you have unknowingly sown along the way, that have been growing all along.

And who the heck is Murphy, anyway?

The Places Where There Are Spaces

I looked it up and do you know what murphy is another name for? A potato. Murphy is a potato! Do you know what is extraordinary about a potato? Every part of it is useful. It can endure through winter storms and grows even in the darkest of cupboards. There is even a movement toward the potato replacing the rose as the symbol of eternal love. And like the potato, we are incredibly resilient and useful and we continue to grow (sometimes especially) in the darkest of times.

So next time you're afraid to jinx something positive or expect something to go wrong, exercise that muscle to receive and hold your good fortune. Not all harvests will produce bumper crops, it's true. But recognizing there's nothing to fear is no small potatoes.

Where in your life might you be telling yourself that it was just luck that got you to where you are today? What might be different if you accepted your good fortune without fear?

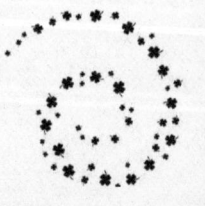

17. The Many Shades of You

When I first started out as a dancer, I prided myself on my bold, dynamic style. I was often complimented for my strength; it's what made me stand out. Ironically, it was also the very thing holding me back from developing as an artist. Early in my career, I moved to NYC to study with my mentor who was the first and only person to tell me in no uncertain terms that I was too strong. Many tears were shed during that period of my training, but I am forever in my mentor's debt for teaching me the invaluable lesson of shading. Through my present lens as a coach, it is not lost on me how it applies to the artistry of life.

In art, shading helps to illustrate depth. In the human experience, shading draws attention and widens perspective to the vast spectrum of emotion and thought available to us as we engage in the ever-changing tempo of life's journey. Different shades allow for juxtaposition. Juxtaposition highlights the nuances, and in the nuances are moments that have spectrums of their own.

Take the color spectrum, for example, the rainbow's natural order: red, orange, yellow, green, blue, indigo, violet. Consider what color you might use to describe yourself. And now, take another moment to consider what color others might use to describe you. What did you notice? If you are like me, I'm guessing that you'll find there is no one color that captures you and that you are unique blend of shades and colors that varies depending on your context.

In our quest to understand who we want to be in the world, how often do we overpower the more nuanced shades of ourselves as I did during my dance training? Are we tapping into only a fraction of the spectrum of colors available to us? According to some estimates, the eye can distinguish more than ten million shades of color.

We tend to label people in order to understand them. Likewise, in our effort to fit in or be understood, we have a propensity to lead with, or present only, one aspect of ourselves in certain situations. So, it's perfectly natural that others may see or define us in just one way, with one color.

I remember once being called a maverick. My first instinct was to reject the notion that I could be associated with such a word. The *Collins English Dictionary* defines a maverick as "a person of independent or unorthodox views." It also points out that it can be used to describe people in both a positive and negative context, which made me feel a little better and piqued my curiosity enough to wonder what others saw in me that I didn't. This exploration allowed me to zoom out and see that it wasn't personal; it's only data, just as

The Places Where There Are Spaces

it was when my mentor told me my dancing was too strong. Could he have been more subtle or nuanced in the way he taught me about shading? *Absolutely!* Nevertheless, when I got curious about how my strength could also be my weakness, it provided me with the very insight I needed to grow.

I am still a strong and powerful dancer, but that's not all that I am. So, I'll take the maverick comment and recognize it as a very small part of the many shades of who I am. I encourage you to do the same and explore the many shades of *you*, and maybe even discover parts of you that have been subdued or overshadowed by your strengths.

What's one aspect or shade of you that you'd like to highlight more in your life?

18. Pivot!

One of my all-time favorite episodes of *Friends* is the one where Chandler and Rachel are enlisted to help Ross move his new couch up the staircase. Despite the fact that the couch clearly won't fit, Ross refuses to believe it and keeps yelling, "Pivot!"

Wedged between the couch and the wall, Chandler cries out for Ross to shut up, and Ross finally concedes: "I don't think it's going to pivot anymore." It makes me laugh out loud every time I think about it.

We can all relate to forcing things when, despite how much we wish they would, they just don't fit. Sometimes, things are just not meant to be, no matter how much you pivot to try and make it work.

In dance, a pivot is a kind of turn. Dancers learn to pivot by developing a strong center to support a change of direction and then to guide it back to the pivot point. If your core is not strong enough, the pivot will be sloppy and throw you off your center.

In life, we pivot all the time, in every waking moment of the day, as we make choices about where and how we choose to engage and experience the things in and around us. The key is to know whether we are making these changes in direction consciously, from our core. It is imperative to draw awareness around the distinction between whether we are being drawn toward something or trying to leave something behind. Or, as in Ross's case, to recognize that no amount of pivoting can make something fit if it just wasn't meant to be.

So, pivot away, my friends, but I encourage you to remember that, just as dancers stretch their muscles and strengthen their core, we must stretch ourselves and become strong enough in our core values so that wherever we pivot, we remain connected to our center.

What deliberate, values-based pivots do you want to make in your life right now?

19. Learning How to Receive

Although many of us are brilliant at finding that perfect gift, why do we sometimes find it so difficult to receive? We've perfected going through the motions when someone gives us something because we know what receiving is "supposed" to look like. We smile and nod with our humble thanks, or maybe even go overboard and gush. Receiving compliments can be even harder. They seem somehow dangerous and summon an instinctual urge to deflect the praise and protect us from being exposed. So, we laugh it off or self-deprecate instead.

But what does receiving *feel* like?

As kids, saying "please" and "thank you" was one of the first things we were taught. Forgetting to say it was also one of the biggest ways we could disappoint our parents. But saying and feeling are not the same thing. It's easy to remember how badly we felt when we were reprimanded for *not* saying it, but did we ever get the chance to experience how giving thanks feels when we genuinely mean it?

There is a gift in receiving. A reciprocal energy that is charged and cyclical. When we give thanks by rote because we are supposed to, rather than taking the time

The Places Where There Are Spaces

to be vulnerable and dig into our hearts to express and share how we really feel, we have stopped the cycle and robbed the giver of the gift—and ourselves—of the joy of receiving. I urge you to slow down and consider how you feel when you receive a gift or a compliment and to express and embody that feeling when you give thanks. Pass it on and pay it forward. And as my gift to you, I offer the words of poet Kahlil Gibran, from his poem "On Pleasure":

Go to your fields and your gardens, and you
shall learn that it is the pleasure of the bee to
gather honey of the flower,
But it is also the pleasure of the flower to
yield its honey to the bee.
For to the bee a flower is a fountain of life,
And to the flower a bee is a
messenger of love,
And to both, bee and flower,
the giving and the receiving of pleasure
is a need and an ecstasy.

—Kahlil Gibran

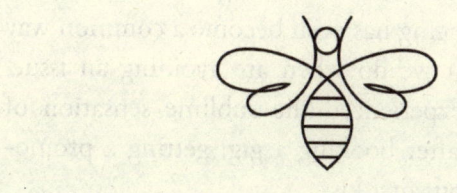

20. The Syncopated Rhythm of Life

We all know how to dance. If you are thinking that this one's about dance and you're not a dancer, *wait*! There is a distinction to be made here and I hope that you'll find it valuable. I repeat. We all know how to dance. We are all dancers. What makes the difference to how we experience our world is understanding whether we are dancing as a means to an end, or if we are in sync with our own rhythm.

Who among us has not found themselves doing the dance in a relationship with a boss, partner, or friend, carefully choreographing each move so we don't step on any toes? How many of us identify with dancing to someone else's tune and losing ourselves in the process? Tap dancing has even become a common way to describe what we do when are avoiding an issue. And we've all experienced the sublime sensation of dancing on air after booking a gig, getting a promotion, or having our first kiss.

As dancers, we focus our training on technique, and often the more proficient we become (number of pirouettes or how high we leap), the further we fall away

The Places Where There Are Spaces

from the essence of what dance is and can be—why we were inspired to dance in the first place.

It's no different in our civilian lives as we line up and fall into formation with the precision of a Radio City Rockette, performing the dance in perfect synchronization with the expectations of everyone else. The more we appear to be dancing or doing on the outside, the less we truly dance inside.

The age clock ticks loudly as it threatens to run out, setting off an alarm as we race against time to dance as much as we can before our bodies fail us. We strain to hear the music inside of us over the cacophony of "shoulds" that overpower the melody that is uniquely our own.

As a dance teacher, I emphasized to my students that "the journey is the thing." I wanted them to understand that, although learning technique is essential, dance isn't something that can be taught, only unleashed.

Dancing takes lifelong mastery and isn't something that I will ever feel a master of; however, it has led me to understand and connect to the infinite pursuit of life mastery. Nowadays, I spend more time in the studio: the studio of my mind, the studio of my heart, and the studio of my values. There, I am fully present as both student and teacher, improvising to the syncopated rhythms of life.

"All that is important is this one moment in movement. Make the moment important, vital, and worth living. Do not let it slip away unnoticed and unused."

—Martha Graham

Reflect on a moment in your life when you felt most in tune with your own rhythm. What made that moment special, and how can you incorporate more of those elements into your present experiences?

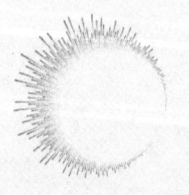

21. The Lies We Tell Ourselves

I woke up yesterday morning to a text message from a client asking me if he could use something powerful that I had said in a session with their own client. Before I had a moment to receive the honor of the request, my egoic mind puffed up with blustery pride. They better credit you if they use your words, it warned me, telling me I that I needed to protect myself and my ideas. It went on to promise me that it was keeping me safe from plagiarism and advised me to hold on very tightly to what was mine.

Something felt horrible in my body, so I just stopped to feel it. I listened to what my body knew, but my mind was too narrowly focused to see. It didn't take long. Just enough time to take in a few breaths was all I needed to feel the warmer, wiser wisdom flow into my mind. From that sage perspective, I was able to recognize that the message from the frightened little voice inside me telling me that I needed to protect myself was untrue. This revelation exposed the tiny-minded thoughts for what they were —lies.

I responded to my client's text by telling him that like good food, we take in the flavor of thoughts, ideas, and experience and mix them together in different measures to make a new recipe bespoke to us. The individual ingredients aren't owned; the recipe is ours to create and recreate.

I extend the same invitation to you, dear reader. By all means, add and share anything you've tasted in my "kitchen" and add your own unique flavor. I went on to suggest that my client serve it—rather than use it—with the people at his table and allow them the opportunity to add their own seasoning.

My client messaged right back and thanked me, saying that I had a way with words. I thanked him for inspiring them.

What lies are you telling yourself that might be holding you back?

22. Carving Out Fresh Paths

My relationship with winter changed profoundly in 2020. The shift coincided with leaving the life I knew and loved as an artist in NYC and heading north to isolate from the impending global pandemic that shut down the world as we knew it.

Winter had been almost nonexistent in the city that year. I remember teaching my last dance class on the ninth of March. It was my birthday and my brilliant musical theater students serenaded me with a rapturous rendition of "Happy Birthday." It was unusually mild, and we enjoyed sitting outside our local Italian bistro for a late-night dinner celebration. Little did we know, it would be the last time we dined in NYC for a very long time.

Fear of the lethal virus spread rapidly—everything changed overnight. The next day, all in-person learning was canceled indefinitely. For dance teachers and students, going remote meant virtual limbo. Classes were suspended until the administration could figure out how to get these dance and theater majors their required studio hours, without access to any studios. Three days later, Broadway shut down.

The Places Where There Are Spaces

We packed up our Hell's Kitchen sublet the next day. We rented a car and headed north to Canada, our home and native land. Decades earlier, we had crossed the international border in the opposite direction, with just a student visa, our beloved cat Ziggy, and dreams of making it in the Big Apple. This time, we identified as New Yorkers and were leaving the country as dual citizens to isolate until "the storm" had passed and we were cleared to return to our former lives.

Winter was alive and well in Quebec. Despite the subzero temperature, a fire rose inside me to rival the warmth of our hearth. It rekindled my creativity and opened my heart and mind. I felt excited and free. That was the season I fell in love with winter.

As kids, we used to pray for a snow day. Do you remember? Hoping for something larger than us to take our fate out of our own hands and cancel school, delay an exam, stop the routine. It was a much-needed permission to slow down and to release the pressures of daily life.

Like a snow day, the pandemic offered us the opportunity to consider where we were going, rather than where we've been. Acknowledging that nothing will ever be the same again is sobering, but waiting for things to return to the way they were is even more detrimental to our mental well-being—pandemic or otherwise.

There are gifts to be found if you dig deep enough to look for them. Like the snow day we wished for when we were kids, we've been given the chance to rethink, to clear our minds, and carve out fresh paths. It's heavy lifting for sure but the great thing about hard work is that you build strong muscles.

So, sleep with a spoon under your pillow, flush ice cubes into the toilet, or wear your pajamas inside out and backward! The season is here to conjure our own storms and create our own permissions. There is no judgement here, only an invitation to see the beauty of this season within you and play in the proverbial snow rather than stay frozen inside waiting for summer to return.

If you had the permission to stop the day-to-day grind, what would you do?

23. Every Day I Make My Bed

Every day, I make my bed. I don't always feel like making it, but still, I make my bed. Some days, the blankets feel heavy and I bang my shin against the frame. Other days, I marvel at the way the sheet catches the air as I shake it out, floating down easily like a parachute making its soft landing.

Either way, I make my bed.

Some days, even though I know I should strip the bed and wash the sheets, I don't take the time or energy to change them. But still, I make my bed.

Other days, I'm so excited to get up that I consider racing out the bedroom door instead. But I slow myself down for a moment. And I make my bed.

Only I know if my bed is messy underneath the top cover that I sometimes smoothly straighten in case someone peeks into my bedroom. Nobody sees me making the bed, and I don't ask for help. At the end of the day, it's my bed and how I make it is entirely up to me. And that is how I'll sleep in it. It won't always be hotel-style perfect, but it's my bed. I am grateful to have a bed.

So, every day, I make my bed.

What's one thing that you can do every day no matter what happens?

24. Unpacking What Weighs Us Down

What would you have to let go of to shed the extra weight that you are carrying right now? I'm not talking about body or physical weight. I'm talking about psychological weight. Is it possible that we have gotten so used to carrying our unprocessed baggage around with us that we've accepted it as a part of who we are?

What would be different if we could put it down?

There's the weight we carry from the past, in memories and regrets, but then there is also the weight that we hold about our unknown future which is often attached to our hopes and fears. Like bags that we overpack with items we think we might need, it is energy spent worrying about something that doesn't exist anymore or hoping for something that hasn't even happened yet.

Like the airlines, there's a price to pay for overweight baggage and it's costing us dearly. We've grown understandably weary from operating this way. The good news is there's a lighter way to travel through life. It's a journey where no baggage is required—you've already got everything you need.

The Places Where There Are Spaces

Let's start unpacking! It's time to be your own travel guide and make a reservation to journey inward to spend some much-needed time with yourself. Let go of any fear or judgement and tap into the excitement of going somewhere new. Remind yourself that, like any new place we go, there are always new things to discover. Get curious. Start to unpack what's in there. Unchecked baggage is often packed so tightly that things get shoved down and we forget why we brought it with us in the first place.

Notice what starts to unfold as you recognize the thoughts, memories, hopes, and fears for what they really are: energy. Your thoughts like everything else are just energy; they aren't directives. You don't need to do anything about them and you certainly don't need to take them with you. We can't control so many things around us, but we can make choices about how we want to travel through this life. We all arrive at the same destination in the end. It's up to us what we experience along the way.

I encourage you to journey inward and unpack the extra weight you've been carrying and to lighten up and enjoy the ride. From where I sit, you've got nothing to lose and everything to gain.

How much time to you spend worrying about things you can't control?

25. Say What You Need to Say

I often wonder why we so often place more value on what others think of us than how we think about ourselves. How is it that we believe that if someone else likes us or what we do or say, then we must be okay? In a world where "likes" are a barometer for whether we are showing up in an acceptable way, we try to please, attract, and impress as many people as we can and then live in fear that someone won't approve or respond in the way we had hoped or expected them to. We've gotten so good at dividing ourselves into smaller and smaller pieces, ending up stretched thin, pleasing no one, with an empty tank. We compound things further by playing relationship politics, often pretending we are okay when we are not and then getting frustrated or even angry when no one notices how we really feel. We've all been there.

At what point did we start to lose our ability to tap into how *we* factor into the equation and instead multiply the distance between who we really are and how we are showing up? Do the math. It doesn't add up. We can't be everything to everybody, but we *can* be everything to ourselves; in fact, we are the only common denominator. The prime number. Whether we feel like it or not, WE are in control. I know that it seems easier sometimes to go with the flow than to share our own thoughts or ideas or to ask for what we want or need, but I promise you, relying on others to define our worth is a zero-sum game. Never ever underestimate how valuable you truly are.

There are more than seven billion people in the world, most of whom will never know you ever existed. And of the ones that do, how many really know you? When you emanate from who you truly are, it isn't important that everyone agrees or likes what you say or do. The important thing is that it matters to *you*! Everyone will not always like what you have to say *and that's okay*! And if they do, that's great too! Either way, you are not defined by the way that they want or expect you to be anymore. It'll be messy and imperfect sometimes, but it'll be yours.

Life is way too short to try and please everyone. The best way you can contribute to the world is by showing up for yourself. And by saying what you need to say, you give permission to others to do the same.

What would you say if you didn't worry about what others think?

26. Our Limitless Capacity to Thrive

Let's face it: feeling unmotivated feels crappy. Especially in a world that places such high value on go-getters. If you are feeling less than inspired at the moment, I promise you there's nothing wrong with you—you aren't broken or weak.

Lack of motivation usually signals a conditional reason for doing something. Whether it's money, praise, success, recognition, control, or power, when something that once motivated us stops being an incentive, it's an opportunity to think again about why we do what we do. It's a chance to connect, reconnect, or maybe even disconnect from what doesn't light us up anymore.

Maybe you've simply grown tired of chasing after something and decided to settle for where you are now. Or maybe when you've been motivated enough to go where you wanted to go, when you got there, it didn't make you feel the way you thought it would.

How many of us have been motivated by fear, the mother of all motivators? When fear is driving us, we're so focused on where we *don't* want to be that we can't even begin to consider where we truly want to go.

The Places Where There Are Spaces

The key here is to understand whether you're being motivated externally, which is limited, or internally, which is limitless. Unconditional, intrinsic motivation feels connected. It doesn't require an outcome to inspire us; the joy is in the process not the result. It doesn't mean you won't get results; in fact, in my coaching practice, I have witnessed that they go hand in hand. As counterintuitive as it may seem, letting go of the win-lose, have–have not perspective brings you even closer to what you want to achieve—and then some!

The distinction between wants and needs is vital to understanding our level of engagement and motivation—or lack thereof—in everything we do.

Needs are things that we require to survive, like food, water, air, and shelter—some of the things we most taken for granted in our modern world. I'm guessing if you are reading this, your basic needs have been met. (It wouldn't hurt to take a conscious moment of gratitude here and put things in perspective.)

Wants are the things that you can live without but would prefer not to. It is the difference between necessity and desire. I'm not talking about greed here; I'm talking about connecting to your purpose, to the reason why you want something. For instance, if you just want to be rich because you want stuff, and you become rich and have stuff, you might find yourself wondering why that didn't satisfy your desire. It's insatiable. It is the reason why people can never have enough of what they don't really need. It's why it's referred to as the hedonic treadmill. When we are motivated by external things and don't consider what's truly important to us and why—aka, what is motivating us intrinsically—then our motivation will be not only unsustainable but what we achieve will cease to bring us joy.

It is a valuable exercise to recognize and appreciate that you already have everything you need and really take stock of what you have that you *don't* really need. Then you can get clear on moving in the direction of what you really want.

As scary and vulnerable as it is to feel uninspired, I invite you to listen deeply to what it's really telling you. Take this moment to slow down and untether your identity from what you do and connect to who you want to be. Leading from our values and finding meaning in what we do is where our limitless capacity to thrive resides.

What truly motivates you?

27. Every Day Is Your Birthday

Our birthday is the one day of the year that we are encouraged—even expected—to brandish our entitlement card, a kind of twenty-four-hour golden ticket to be selfish and indulgent. Honestly, shouldn't we be celebrating the mother who bore us? So, we plan our birthdays accordingly—with all the associated expectations and attachments—simultaneously setting the stage with clichés of what self-care looks like from the outside, while on the inside, we quietly keep score of how others are celebrating us.

It was my birthday, and I woke up with all the preconceived notions of how I was supposed to feel, along with the high expectations for how others were supposed to make me feel. I resisted the urge to check my social media and feed my ego with the puffed-up proof that I am "liked" and made myself a cup of tea instead. My husband had left a card propped up on the kitchen counter, and I smiled, thinking to myself that he always finds the funniest cards. My smile was quickly interrupted by the intrusive judgemental voice of the scorekeeper in my head that said, *Yeah, but no*

The Places Where There Are Spaces

flowers? I took a deep breath. I was proud of myself for calling the thought out for what it was—just a thought—and disempowered its hold on me by replacing it with a thought that served me better.

I moved into the living room to do my morning reading. To my delight, my husband had made me a fire. Score! Take that unwanted voice in my head! Wait, who's playing the score keeping game now? I sat down cross-legged on the floor with my book and my cup of tea, feeling the warmth of the flame on my back. *Life is good*, I thought. I noticed that the humidifier was on; he must have filled it up for me! He knows how the fire dries out my skin, how thoughtful of him. *Big score!* I'm so fortunate, I told myself, and was effusive with my gratitude for his knowing just what I needed. When he told me that it was not him who did that, my scorekeeper was in its element. The thoughts came crashing in. Disappointed, I thanked him for the fire and the card (read: two out of three points) and reached for my phone.

I repeat: life is made up of moments and each moment is what you make it. In that moment, I allowed myself to be led by all the limiting beliefs of what a happy birthday is supposed to look like and, instead of reading, which would have brought me joy in that moment, I resorted to looking for external validation.

The birthday wishes were coming in at quite a pace already and, out of the thirty-six or more people so far, there were less than three that I could even recognize or tell you anything about. "If you can't say something nice, don't say anything at all" came into my head and I wondered if just saying something nice without any associated true connection is worse than not saying anything at all. I started to think about the people I hadn't heard from yet, setting up more expectations for the people I care about. Why do we do that?

Why do we set the bar so high for others to celebrate us and so low for celebrating ourselves? Why can't we believe that we deserve to be celebrated the other 364 days of the year? How can we expect others to celebrate us if we don't celebrate ourselves—everyday. If I am counting the conditional things that are met as wins, and my saboteur scorekeeping voice is keeping track of expectations that are not met, isn't that the same thing? What would be different if we showed up for ourselves instead of relying on others to prove our worth?

By the end of that day, there were over two hundred "Happy birthday" wishes and, though it was nice to be remembered, I felt more grateful for the reminder that at the end of the day, it is up to me to celebrate and honor myself.

Let's consider each day our birthday and celebrate ourselves every day.

Where in your life are you seeking external validation to feel worthy?

28. Pages Left Unturned

We've all felt the allure of trying something new. A novel idea or aspirational thought that bubbles up inside us, tempting us to wonder what it feels like on the other side of our comfort zone. Skimming the surface of possibility, we meander there for a while, like we do in the aisles of a bookstore that has drawn us in with its rows of wisdom, enticing us to let go of looking at our world in the same old way, daring us to learn, to grow, to dream. We rarely allow ourselves to stay there very long and instead retreat to the safety of what we already know. It's easy to buy the book. It's not as easy to read it. Why do you suppose that is? It's not that the words are difficult, or that we don't understand its value, so why is it so hard to follow through with what in that fleeting moment felt so exciting? Why, if we know logically that growth is good for us, do we so often just stay right where we are, or even defer to others while we watch from the sidelines?

My daughter recently gave me a book that inspired me to write this today. I imagine her alone in the bookstore carefully selecting a title that she knows will delight me. She is an expert at giving and seems to find

The Places Where There Are Spaces

immense joy in it, yet she is a complete novice when it comes to giving to herself. I have no doubt that I will immerse myself in the prose of the beautiful book she gave me and, ironically, highlight passages that I hope might resonate with her. Although she chose the book, I know she won't read it, and it pains me to know that the very thing that might help her is just beyond a page unturned.

Have you ever considered how many pages have been left unturned in your life, things you've thought about but never tried? How many books line your shelves waiting patiently to offer you a passage to a new way of thinking—unworn and unshared, bursting with possibility—just beyond the cover.

We are so much closer to wonder and transformation than we know. But if these possibilities continue to remain in our blind spot, as time inevitably passes, they may someday only appear in our rearview mirror. Whether it's exploring the boundaries of a relationship, a project you are working on, a career change, or a literal book you've been wanting to read, I encourage you to open it up and start turning the pages. It doesn't matter if you finish it; it just matters that you begin. One insight can change everything. You never know where your next chapter might take you.

A moment of clarity without any action is just a thought that passes in the wind. But a moment of clarity followed by an action is a pivotal moment in our life.

—Don Miguel Ruiz

What's one thing that has been sitting on the shelf that you can start today?

29. The Power of Soup

Every once in a while, I make soup. I don't follow a recipe and the soups I make are never the same. Often, the goal is not so much to make soup as it is to clean out the fridge. And yet, each time I do it, as the ingredients start to simmer and the savory smells waft through the air, I am reminded how powerful soup making can be.

Unassuming and generous in its simplicity, the soup gradually evolves as the hours pass and the ingredients intermingle to co-create a new flavor that improves over time. We find ourselves being drawn into the kitchen, eager to consume. But it isn't ready yet, so we commune instead. We gather around the soup's steady patient simmer, a gentle reminder to slow down and take our time. We discuss flavors and laugh as we playfully debate which spices might improve or detract from the concoction. What began as a chore is now a collaboration as we share a taste from the same spoon. What started out as scarcity has become abundant in its gifts.

The alchemy of soup is in the transformation of what seems like useless scraps of unwanted leftovers into something that has the power to draw us together, stimulate our creativity, and nourish our souls.

So, the next time you tell yourself you don't have the ingredients you need to create something new—or look inside your proverbial fridge and tell yourself there's nothing to eat—I challenge you to discover that the recipes are yours to create and promise that you've got everything you need right now.

What is holding you back right now from creating something new?

30. The Wisdom of Wordle

Yesterday morning, for the very first time, I used up all my attempts to figure out the right five-letter word in Wordle, a game I play every morning. Until yesterday, I could always guess the correct word before I ran out of tries. If you aren't familiar with the game, no worries. I'm guessing the Wordle Wisdom will resonate just the same.

Usually, I take about five minutes to complete the game, share my results with our Wordle group, and go on with my day. But this day was different. Not only did I not guess the correct word quickly, but I also quickly used up all my chances and still didn't get the right word. I didn't labor over it as I was doing it; I always find the answer and take pride in the fact that I place little value on whether I complete it in the least number of turns. But I hadn't ever considered what it would feel like if I couldn't complete it at all.

The rules of the game are simple: you get six attempts to guess a five-letter word. A green tile means you have the right letter in the right place, a yellow tile means the letter is in the word but in the wrong place, and the dreaded gray tile means you guessed a letter

The Places Where There Are Spaces

that's not in the word at all. The game begins when you choose your first word.

According to the Free Dictionary, there are 158,390 words with five letters. Volume 6 of the Scrabble dictionary claims there are 8,996. Either way, the sky is pretty much the limit when you begin, so long as it is a verifiable five-letter word.

You can learn a lot about yourself in that first moment of choice. When faced with endless possibilities of how to begin or play the game, what criteria do you use to choose? Does the fear of five grays (no right answers) in your opening move factor into how you choose your first move? And, if you do happen to get five grays, as I have many times, will that trigger you into a scarcity mindset: Oh no, I only have five turns to get it right! or one of self-loathing: I'm horrible at this? Or will you embrace a growth mindset, knowing that what's not in the right answer is just as valuable information as knowing what is?

Endless possibilities, a blank slate. Take a chance and choose a word that means something to you. Yesterday, I chose *heart* and was off to a great start, guessing two letters that were in the word, but in the wrong position (two yellows, three grays). Next, I used my logical brain and positioned the E and the R at the end with the word *power*. That gave me three out of five letters all in the correct position and only my second guess! What happened next was interesting.

With my confidence bias in full gear, for the next four turns, I easily chose words that fit the criteria, but none of them were the "right" answer. I still only had three out of the five letters solved: *loner, joker, coder.* With just one last go left, I typed my final guess: *boxer.* It's got to be the one! I said to myself. Then I stopped. Before I pushed enter on my last guess, I slowed down for a moment to consider the fact that although it was likely the correct answer (yup, still living into my confidence bias), I was curious about what happens when you "fail" to solve the puzzle since I never had. So, without trepidation and unattached to the outcome, I pushed enter and, lo and behold, I was wrong again.

The correct answer popped up on the screen: *foyer.* In that moment when I "lost" the game for the first time, something inside of me opened up. I stared at the word and smiled. I have had the great privilege of standing in some of the finest foyers in theaters around the world. A foyer is an entrance, an opening, something to pass through, a portal. A gathering place before we pass through. It is not an end but an entry point to new possibilities, and, like a portal, my "failure to win" inspired me to write this today.

So, thank you, Wordle, for reminding me that there is an infinite number of new beginnings and an endless array of possibilities that lie beyond having the right answer. There will be another game tomorrow and the next day and the day after that. How we play it is entirely up to us.

What might be different if you got curious,
instead of upset, when you don't win?

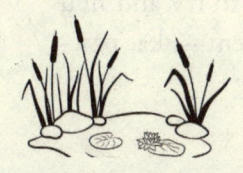

31. Lessons from a Snake

Just the other morning, I looked one of my fears in the eye. Well, not exactly the eye—that is a little too brave for me in this instance. Let's just say I slowed down long enough to face my fear instead of allowing it to trigger my knee-jerk default reaction. It wasn't exactly easy, and I wouldn't go so far as to say I have conquered my fear, but I can safely say that I learned something about fear, and for that, I am grateful.

It was a glorious spring morning and I had just returned from my first kayak of the season. I felt the early morning sun warming my face, and my loyal heartbeat returning to its resting rhythm after our spirited paddle on the lake. It was great to be alive, I thought, taking a sip from my coffee and opening my book as I settled in for my morning reading.

Moments later, my flow was interrupted by something moving in my peripheral. I looked up from my book to find a very long snake in the grass. My first instinct was to bolt or jump up on my chair and scream! But instead, I coached myself to try and find the gift and opportunity in that moment—aka, practice what I preach.

The Places Where There Are Spaces

It's not uncommon to have a fear of snakes. I suppose you might even be able to divide people neatly into two groups: fearless and downright terrified. I fall in the latter. But I'm starting to discover that fear isn't so binary as that.

When we identify ourselves as being one way or the other (think: creative/not creative, funny/not funny, city person/country person) we limit ourselves to a wide array of other ways to experience or look at things. We aren't taking into consideration context or leaving ourselves open to new possibilities. I have no lived data to support my fear of snakes other than what's been learned or passed down through the media. I've never encountered one (because I've always avoided places where I might see them or opportunities to learn more about them because I put myself in the I'm-afraid-of-snakes camp). If your perspective is that you are not creative, it is unlikely that you'll look for opportunities that invite creativity.

I wish I could report that I am so enlightened that I noticed the snake and then just went on reading, but instead, I stopped reading entirely and slowly put my book down, hoping the snake wouldn't see me. As I write this, I laugh at myself. Funny how, especially in fear, we think of ourselves as the very center of the universe.

It turns out that snakes can barely see which is why they stick out their tongues to sense where they are. The notion that the snake was looking at me is as ludicrous as it is impossible! The snake was taking absolutely no notice of me as it gently slithered through the grass looking for grubs. I imagine with all the predators around it probably had some legitimate fears of its own!

I took a few deep breaths and got the courage to look more closely at the snake. I remarked on how long it was, noticing the two yellow stripes down its back and its forked tongue flickering. I felt surprisingly peaceful for a moment in its company, despite my brain trying to hijack my thoughts with images of *Indiana Jones* and the snake pit, conjuring up all sorts of horrors. I gently guided myself back to the moment. Just then, the snake moved closer and stopped not far from where I was sitting—to bask in the sun just as I had been doing. It occurred to me that we were sharing an experience: the same sun, the same earth, the same moment in time. There was something almost sacred about it, and I felt wistful as I watched him slither away into the bush.

Later that day, I did my due diligence to find out what kind of a snake it was, just to make sure it wasn't dangerous. I discovered that the garter snake is harmless and happens to be a welcome companion to the gardener because they eat grubs.

I'm still wary of snakes and I'm not gonna lie, I'm more inclined to wear shoes in the garden than I was before. I'm no longer in the terrified-of-snakes camp though, and I might even learn to call my garter snake my friend. The next time I sit out in my garden and feel the sun on my face, I will be reminded of our encounter and the lessons I learned from a snake that day.

What is something you fear that you might not actually be as scary as you think?

32. Taking the Pressure off Flow

There has been an entire industry developed around flow. The word that once described a quality of movement has *become* a movement in a stressed-out world desperate to find meaning and life purpose—a "raison d'être."

We are inundated daily by reminders of how great flow is. Our literal and metaphorical inboxes are OVERflowing with the latest directions on how to get there. And, although I think it would be fair to say that most of us consider flow to be a desirable state in which to reside, if you have ever felt frustrated or overwhelmed in your quest to find or arrive at flow, you are most definitely not alone.

Despite what the billion-dollar mindfulness industry promises, flow is not a destination. No mantra, mindfulness program, or affirmation will get you there, and there certainly is no one-size-fits-all for every occasion. This is your invitation—your permission—to ease up and take the pressure off flow.

Imagine for a moment that you are a garden hose and your garden is your world—everything you've created and experienced up until now. It is composed

The Places Where There Are Spaces

of the things that you put energy into and grow and nurture, as well as things that you try to keep alive, even though perhaps they've had their season. Some things in your garden flourish with little oversight needed, like perennials with strong roots that brave through even the harshest of seasons. Others require more special care and attention. Some things will even cross-pollinate and grow new into new things without you ever even knowing.

In this analogy, water is your energy, your flow. The nozzle is your mind, which controls all your settings or filters—the thoughts and associated emotions that direct your energy, responses, and choices.

Flow is limitless, and all intensities serve us, depending on the context. Like the garden hose, we can adjust the flow and reduce, or intensify the pressure, depending on what we want or need. There is no one setting for all the things that you grow in your garden, and what might require more pressure in certain climates may need less in others. The key is to know that it is you that has the power to control the different settings. Kinks in the hose show up in our lives as limiting beliefs, assumptions, interpretations, and fear, and threaten to reduce our potential to access our natural flow and drain our energy. But remember *we* are the hose and, just as we create our garden, it is only us that constricts our flow.

There will be times when you feel like you need to protect what you are growing in your garden from pests or saboteurs by building fences. There will also be instances when you opt to remove the barriers and expand the garden. And there will be times when you experience a dry spell, and no matter how much you try, you can't find your flow, and that is perfectly okay. Just because you aren't flowing doesn't mean you are not growing.

Like water, our flow is our own renewable resource. It can be used inward for personal growth and outward for whatever it is we want to create or grow.

What is something you'd like to grow?

33. What Are You Tolerating?

What are you putting up with right now that never used to bother you at all? Think about it. Are there people, habits, or things in your life that are draining your energy more than filling you up at this moment? Are there people, habits, or things in your life that used to light you up but just don't in the same way they used to? And, instead of reading the signs—the exhaustion, overwhelm—do you desperately try to adjust and accommodate? Or perhaps you tolerate the discomfort because you have convinced yourself that it must be you. Deep breath, I know this is hard, but we can do hard things. (Thank you, Glennon Doyle.)

It is so much easier to blame ourselves than to confront the truth or hurt someone's feelings and risk feeling vulnerable or ending up alone. And so we explain away the discomfort we feel by trying to adapt, accommodate, and contort ourselves for others instead. It feels safer that way. Better to avoid than to feel judged, embarrassed, guilty, or shamed. So, we tolerate. We carry the burden of external things we feel like we can't control or change. We take away from

The Places Where There Are Spaces

ourselves to show up for others, rather than face what we really know deep down inside.

If only we would listen.

If fear is a mask for desire, then toleration is a cover-up for fear. A kind of protective armor we create to keep ourselves safe from the things on the outside that might hurt us. Heavy and impermeable, our armor gives us the illusion that we can't be hurt from the outside, but it doesn't address the underlying discomfort that stays locked inside of us because we can't—or won't—allow ourselves to let it out. Although it may feel like the lesser of the evils, toleration is unsustainable.

Toleration is also as close as you ever come to your edge, to true enlightenment, to freedom. But you'll never be able to know what's on the other side of toleration unless you are willing to risk vulnerability, uncertainty, guilt, and shame, and live into what you know deep down, to what you *feel* inside to be the truth.

There needs to be a real audit right now of what external stuff is blocking our energy. We do so much work internally that we sometimes mistake that to mean we are obligated to take on all the responsibility, to adjust course when things shift externally, instead of being okay with adjusting our own course if things aren't working the way they used to or the way we want them to. We berate ourselves when old habits don't produce the same results.

When do favorite things change from anchor to ball-and-chain, holding you down rather than steadying or centering you, becoming something you put up with rather than address? What are you tolerating right now that cannot be transformed back to something that energizes you? How often have you tried adjusting course but still it feels more like bailing out water in a sinking vessel just to keep things afloat? How much blame and guilt are you putting on yourself right now to continue doing what you've committed to do—holding on to what you think you need when the truth is you've outgrown it? When will you realize it doesn't fit anymore?

It takes courage to think about these questions, but I know you've got this. Behind your protective armor of toleration and underneath the fear, lies what you really want. I promise you it isn't nearly as scary or far away as it seems. It's time to come home again to nurture and reevaluate what is best for your own growth, inside and out.

What are you tolerating that you'd rather let go of?

34. First Thoughts and Overwhelm

There is a space between the moment you wake up and the first thought that you have. A space ripe with possibility, when the body is just that little bit ahead of the mind. It is a peaceful, clear, wide-open space—a visceral place, where words and time don't exist, and feeling and instinct reside.

But as the mind starts to wake up, that very same space begins to fill with that first thought, which leads to the next thought you have and the subsequent thoughts that you generate about those thoughts—ranking, evaluating, fighting, or suppressing them. The brain has been aroused, and like a tipped-over bottle of milk, the thoughts come rushing in and spilling over before you've even set your feet on the floor. Once again, you are back in the race, already behind and still needing to clean up the mess. Sound familiar?

Operating this way is the perfect recipe for overwhelm. It is living a life fueled by the limited, unsustainable energy of stress. And don't disregard the energy you expend stressing about the mess. Before you know it, the notion that things are a mess transforms into *I'm a mess*, ultimately attributing the word to who you are

The Places Where There Are Spaces

as a person by calling yourself a mess and so on. You get the idea.

So, what do we do about it?

Well, let's first look at what mess means to you. How do you define messy? Where did you learn that definition? Does your current mess really need to be cleaned up? And if so, why? Why is that important to you? Where is that message coming from? Who decides what's messy or messed up?

Did you know that Albert Einstein was reported to have been a very messy person? When others criticized his unsightly work habits, he retorted: "If a cluttered desk is a sign of a cluttered mind, then what are we to think of an empty desk?"

But it isn't about whether you are tidy or messy in your external world; it's the thought messiness that most affects us and makes it difficult to process and focus. A cluttered mind can be disruptive. It hinders our productivity, balance, and ultimately our mental health.

Remember that space between the moment we wake up and the first thought that we have? Our first thought is one of the most pivotal because it sets the course of our day. Knowing that can be a superpower. Pre-programmed default thoughts and limiting beliefs will rush into that space like that bottle of spilled milk as the mind wakes up vigilantly trying to protect you from failing—filling the space with thoughts and lies to motivate you like: *You are already behind, You are lazy!* and *You are a mess!*—using any means necessary to scare you into action.

But you don't need fear to motivate you. Like a Ninja Warrior, your strength is in your *lack* of fear which provides you with the determination and strength you need to operate at your highest potential. You can be ready for those energy-draining counterproductive thoughts by preparing an alternate first thought that sets you up for a successful and energized day. What's a thought that might serve you better? Practice that thought. Practice it until it becomes natural. Oh, and regarding the mess part? Tidy or messy—who cares! That proverbial bottle of spilt milk that we race to clean up is the same one that the cat laps up, reveling in its good fortune. And fun fact: while the exact origin of the idiom "Don't cry over spilt milk" isn't exactly known, it is said to come from faery lore. Whenever milk was spilled, it was considered a little extra offering to the fairies and nothing to worry about.

What might be a first thought that would help you start your day off right?

35. The Call from Your Inner Agent

At sixteen, while sitting on the floor of my high school hallway, I was visited by a thought. A thought so crystal clear there was no room or need to debate. It appeared from out of nowhere. Unaccompanied by hubris or bravado, it declared itself to me as a matter-of-fact knowing, an indisputable truth that was mine to behold should I choose to believe it—and I did. *You can do it.*

Rather than understanding what the broader message was, as I do now, like any other self-centered teenager, I assigned its meaning to something that was specific and relevant to me. Because I was interested in dance at the time, I took it to mean that I was going to pursue dance. And pursue dance I did, fueled by an inner knowing that I could do it.

In my lifelong career as a performing arts professional, I have never had an agent. But in that seminal moment when I was visited by this undeniable thought, my own agency was born. What I was given that day was a glimpse of what was possible if I set my mind to it. It felt differently than being driven by passion or ambition—although I had plenty of that too—but in that moment, it was the simple realization that if I wanted to do something, I could do it. At the time, it aligned with my desire to dance and so I attached my agency to the pursuit of that dream. Now, I realize that agency is not attached to what I'm doing, only who I am *being* in whatever I do.

People have often remarked on my confidence, some even attributing it to knowing how to hold myself because I was a dancer, others ascribing my inner strength to being influenced by the hardness of NYC. To me, it never felt cold or calculating, but always warm and nurturing, sometimes bubbling with possibility other times simmering with resolve.

Agency helps us maintain a sense of control in our life. It strengthens our ability to shape our thoughts and actions and helps us stay the course during challenging or changing times.

Like all of us, my attention can be hijacked sometimes by all the noise and negative energy that exists in our world. But I have vowed to listen instead to the louder, clearer voice of my inner agent. I don't—let me rephrase that—I *won't* take for granted that I have had an ally inside me all this time championing and supporting me in everything I do, no matter how big or small. Even in the toughest of times, I hear its voice loud and clear, reminding me that I am capable, because it is me who influences and creates my own thoughts.

I am eternally grateful to have listened to the message from my agent all those years ago. I truly believe that we all have an agent inside us waiting to be heard, ready to co-create the life we envision. So, if you haven't heard from your agent lately, be sure to check your messages.

What do you know will stay true about you no matter what happens?

36. What Do You Want to Be When You Grow Up?

I was in the grocery store with my newborn baby girl in my shopping cart, safely tucked in her baby carrier, facing me with her eyes wide open, as they so often were. I chatted with her as we went up and down the aisles gathering our groceries—"Maybe I should make soup," "Do you think we need more pasta?"—speaking to her in normal tones as I would any other fellow human being.

More than a quarter of a century ago now, I can still clearly recall the attitude of the man who turned around from the other side of the aisle that day and asked me rather indignantly who I was talking to. I have no idea whether he noticed there was a baby in my cart, but it was crystal clear that I had disturbed him. He either thought I was crazy—keep in mind this was before Bluetooth or cell phones and way before calling somebody crazy was considered stigmatizing—or that I had no business talking to a baby. Whichever it was, he was rudely confronting me, and I could feel the mama bear effect rising in me with indignation to rival his own. Although I felt like reading him the riot act on "baby-ism" and asking him who he thought he

The Places Where There Are Spaces

was talking to, I calmly told him that I was speaking to my daughter.

For the most part, when we were babies, the adults in our orbit rarely spoke directly to us. They were particularly good at talking *about* us while we were there, assuming we couldn't understand, like foreigners who don't speak the language. What they neglected to realize, however, was that although we didn't have language, we were superior readers of body language and highly attuned to sensing feelings, attitudes, and energy; our lives depended on it. We listened to and noticed everything. Each moment was an opportunity to learn, and we'd try and experience our life instead of trying to make sense out of it as adults so often do.

As we got a little bit older, the adults in our lives seemed more interested in what we were able to do. Whether it was our parents wanting to show us off—"Sammy, show your grandmother how you can sing, jump, or do your ABC's"—or a relative or family friend that wanted to be the first to get us to say or do something and then report it—"Look! Susie's really good at this!"

You get the idea.

And so, in our formative years, we performed instead. Like beloved pets, we delighted and impressed them with our accomplishments, our wit, our talent and beauty. And it worked. The rewards were rich. We felt loved and accepted, and so we attached meaning to these encounters.

The adults in our lives were the first ones to assign labels to who we are in order that they might understand or explain us—"She's shy," "He's spirited"—and because we were children, we accepted those labels as part of us because the people that were labeling us were the very same ones keeping us alive. And so, we stopped looking to discover or create who we were, and our limiting beliefs were born.

And then we learned to say no. A foreshadowing of the rebellious teenager in us, sometimes, we said no because we didn't want something, but other times we felt like saying no was the only thing that felt like we had any control over.

Around five years old or so, when we finally learned to speak, the adults in our life started asking us, "What do you want to be when you grow up?" Sometimes we took this as an opportunity to dream, but most of the time, we felt like we should know the answer already. And so, we created answers that made the people we loved and relied on smile or laugh or brag about how clever we were, searching for the answer that would elicit a response that made us feel safe. The pride on their faces when we said things they could understand or repeat at a cocktail party—"I want to be a doctor, lawyer, teacher"—was in stark contrast to the fear that registered when we said something that was foreign to them or sounded unattainable or flighty. Worse yet, when we floated an actual dream that we had—"I want to be a hockey player, dancer, astronaut"—they'd be so supportive that it felt more like an obligation than a

The Places Where There Are Spaces

dream. Their enthusiasm, while well-intentioned, was overwhelming and followed by an avalanche of support that filled up our schedules with lessons, practices, and platitudes about hard work.

And so it goes that, for a brief time, we were living a life of infinite possibilities, believing wholeheartedly that we could be anything we dreamed. Until all the things we thought we could be turned into *should be*—which I like to say is could with shame. And eventually, we find ourselves as adults doing all the things but not taking the time to ask ourselves why.

The good news: it's never too late to ask yourself that most important follow-up question so often omitted when we are first asked what we want to be when we grow up: Why is that important to you? Your *why* is your inner compass and exactly where your values reside. When you take into consideration why you are attracted to something, you may find that there are other things that share that quality or reason. For instance, if I were to ask myself all those years ago why pursuing dance or theater was important to me, I might have discovered that it goes deeper than because I'm good at it or it seems like fun. My first career in the performing arts and my second career as a coach share more similarities that resonate with my purpose than I might have imagined.

So, take a moment and ask yourself who you want to be and why that is important to you. The answer is there, if you listen. No words required.

Who do you want to be in the world and why is that important to you?

37. Portals to Possibilities

Have you ever found yourself someplace and had the realization that nobody has any idea of where you are? It's not a lost feeling, but rather a thrilling sensation, a kind of freedom. Anonymous and unburdened by where you've been or where you are going, completely in the moment and untethered to the expectations of what it is supposed to be. Your senses come alive, and your analytical mind is eclipsed by your heart center that is now wide open and basking in the present with no need to assign meaning to it. You feel simply delighted and grateful that you are there. These kinds of moments cannot be planned. They aren't on any agenda or itinerary and, like gateways or portals, can transport you to places you never imagined you would go when you woke up that morning.

I had just such an experience during our first visit back to NYC since the pandemic. We'd been gone more than two years away that we always thought we'd never have a good enough reason to leave. What started out as a morning stroll with my coffee that day, transformed into an experience that I never would have imagined. The cultural aspect of the experience was exquisite, and there are plenty of things I might share in that regard, but what stood out to me more in that moment was the deeper awareness around how much magic there is just beyond our daily routines. The only reason I ended up where I did that morning was that a portal opened and I stepped through.

We were staying directly across the street from Lincoln Center, and when I saw that the New York City Ballet was opening their season that night, I thought it'd be a great idea to get tickets. It had been so long since we had seen any live performances. While waiting for the box office to open, an elderly woman approached me. *She's probably a volunteer usher*, I thought to myself. It's funny how we assume things about people. For all I knew she was one of the big donor patrons of the ballet. "Are you here for rehearsal?" she asked me, mistaking me for one of the musicians. I told her that we were there to buy tickets for the ballet that evening, and I couldn't help but notice how her assumption made me feel.

Maybe it was my long absence from the city that had me questioning my identity. The notion that she thought I was one of the players somehow validated me. It put some wind in my sails as I strutted through Lincoln Center Plaza, feeling more like the artist I've always been than the tourist I was that day. It had been two and a half years since I was living and working in NYC. I was feeling all the feels. Even my coffee tasted better. I recognize now that I was holding onto the limiting belief that being away from the city for so long somehow devalued my credibility.

The Places Where There Are Spaces

Fifteen minutes later, we wandered back to see if the box office was open yet and noticed that the door was ajar and there were some people filing in. I asked someone if the box office was open. They nodded yes and we crossed through. Portal #1.

Curiosity kicked in as I noticed a few people heading left into the lobby of the theater rather than straight ahead to the box office. Even though it was clearly a private event, I followed them and went left instead. It was exhilarating. Just then, I heard someone behind me say, "Excuse me," and I turned to see a security person approaching me. "Excuse me," he said again, coming closer. *This is it*, I thought, bracing myself to be banished from Lincoln Center. I stood there frozen, my heart racing faster the closer he got. "I'm sorry," he said, "but you can't take your coffee past here." My coffee! He had no idea that I was an imposter! I took a deep breath and thanked him for the reminder as I handed over my coffee. He then unhooked the red velvet stanchion and we confidently passed through. Portal #2.

Up ahead, I could see people giving their names to someone standing at a lectern who was checking names off a list. *Of course*, I thought. *The orchestra rehearsal—this must be an invited rehearsal.* The next moment could absolutely have been perceived as an obstacle. I might even have opted to play it safe and walk away. (It's certainly what my husband was hoping I'd do, if the terrified look in his eyes as he followed me were any indication.) I ignored the urge to run and approached the gatekeeper confidently. I mentioned something about us knowing someone in the opera and, even though we were not on the list, he added our names and invited us through. Portal #3.

I had no idea when I woke that morning that, just hours later, I'd be sitting in the balcony at Lincoln Center's David Koch Theater watching a closed orchestra rehearsal for the opening night of the New York City Ballet. As the conductor raised his baton, a sacred, focused quiet came over all who were in the hall that morning. In that silence, I felt simultaneously anonymous and connected to myself and everyone else. It was true that nobody in the world who knew me had any idea of where I was. But I did.

These kinds of moments stand out because they are rarer than they need to be. The irony is they aren't unicorn occurrences, they aren't so difficult to find. Life never stops offering us the chance to dance, but so often, we are unaware of the invitation, or worse yet, we get a glimpse but decline the offer, choosing to stand on the sidelines instead. It's like stumbling on a treasure chest and not opening it because you don't have the time or walking away because it might be too hard or scary. With practice, we can become more aware of what is available to us and create more of these moments in our lives. I invite you to be open to seeing them as more than random moments and take the time and develop the courage to see and pass through the portals to possibilities.

The Places Where There Are Spaces

That night, I went back to the opening night of the ballet as a ticketed audience member. It was exquisite. I closed my eyes and felt gratitude for the portals that were offered to me earlier that day and for the courage to step through them. The theater was filled now with well-dressed patrons of the arts who, unlike me, very clearly wanted to be noticed. As the conductor raised his baton, I listened to the orchestra play its first notes remembering how wonderful it felt to be anonymous.

Try going somewhere you've been before and look for things along the way that you never noticed before. What did you discover?

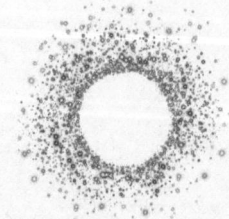

38. How Stepping Away from Your Work Makes You More Productive

Every morning, whenever possible, I like to write before I start my day. I don't eat first, because the hunger I feel at this time of day can only be satiated by creativity. That's the best kind of hunger. Some mornings, I am simply not inspired to write, either because I've sabotaged my muse by checking my email or socials first, or maybe I feel like writing but can't seem to focus my attention on what—a kind of paralysis by analysis. As humans, we thrive when we are working hard and flounder when we are hardly working. We tend to put a lot of pressure on ourselves to be constantly innovating and creating or learning something new, to always be productive, and when we aren't, we feel somehow less than or not up to par.

The word "work" has become associated with reward or acknowledgement—so much so that there's even a new word in the Urban Dictionary "werk," defined as a congratulatory exclamation of approval.

When our usual ways of doing things aren't working, we convince ourselves that something must be wrong with us. We have the data to support it too. We've done it before, so why can't we do it now? Glimpses of imposter syndrome start to creep in as we create stories about the reasons why. *It was a fluke last time, I'm a one-shot wonder.* We berate ourselves with negative thoughts that distract us and deviate from the original goal and waste our energy by creating anxiety and distress instead. If the negative self-talk isn't enough to paralyze us, we shift into troubleshooting mode and attempt to "fix" the situation by trying harder, working longer, forcing ourselves to produce. But it's even harder now, because now we are spending our energy on trying to fix something that we perceive as a problem.

But hold on a second! There's nothing to fix. There is *no* problem. You haven't suddenly lost it. There is nothing wrong with you. Take a moment to step back and breathe. Your creativity hasn't gone anywhere; it's always been there. It's *you* that has departed. You are off on some tangent creating volumes of stories, explanations, and excuses about why things aren't working, why *you* aren't working. Getting further and further away from engaging in the very thing you wanted to do in the first place! What's interesting here is that we have stumbled upon a tool that can be quite useful if we are aware enough to choose it rather than default to it via a stress response.

Take another moment to consider how much time you waste trying to be more productive and then discover you are even further away from what you are

The Places Where There Are Spaces

trying to do. What would be different if instead of spending time and energy trying to force productivity, you chose to step away, to create space between you and the goal?

Distancing ourselves, when used as a tool, affords us the space and perspective we sometimes need to renew our energy. Think about a time when you had forced perspective, when you had to sit out of a performance because of injury or illness. Do you recall how amazing it felt to return when you felt better?

Our days are filled with these opportunities to step away, even in a micro-moment, and widen our lens so we can access more of our higher frequencies and focus on what it is we really want to be doing.

I have lots of unfinished ideas and I'm okay with that; I know they'll wait for me. In fact, I do some of my best work in places I would never associate with working. Don't limit yourself by believing ideas only get done in some cloistered workspace. That's just the place where you record the work. The work is created inside of you. Wherever you are.

Where in your life would stepping away help you renew your energy?

39. How Did You Get Here?

You can keep on keeping on doing what you are doing right now. You are already here. You have arrived at this place in space and time, and it was you who got yourself here. There may have been external factors in play, and obstacles that you've had to overcome, but at the end of the day, it is you who has made a series of decisions that led you to where you are in your life right now. And, depending on what lens you are looking through at this moment, what you do next is determined by how you choose to look at things right now. Think about it. What factors played into you being at this point of your life right now?

How did you get here?

Let's step away from the big existential question for a minute and simply look at this small moment in time right now that we're sharing together. Take a moment to breathe and center yourself. Just continue breathing as you scan your body. Notice any tension you are feeling and simply breathe into that area and let it go. Breathe in for 4-3-2-1, hold for 1-2, and release for 5-4-3-2-1.

Let me ask you something: Why are you reading this right now? Was it planned? Is it because you always do? Did you stumble upon the book and get curious or maybe someone told you that you should check it out? Think about it. What was it that led you to being here in this moment right now? Whatever your reason, you have arrived here and chosen to be here reading my words. You also have a choice to stop listening to me. You can simply close your eyes or put the book back on the shelf or shut down the e-reader. Go ahead and try it and just listen to what thoughts flood into your brain. I'll be here when you return, and I hope that you do, but if you decide not to, it's totally okay. It's entirely up to you. So, when I say go, stop reading for thirty seconds and just pay attention to your thoughts. 5-4-3-2-1, GO.

What did you notice?

When we allow ourselves the space to think more consciously about *what* we are doing and connect to *why* we are doing them, it offers us the opportunity to consider *how* we want to do them. It increases our engagement and helps us to distinguish whether we are doing things by choice, because they serve us, or default, because it's what we are used to.

You can keep on doing things the way you've always done them. You already know how. You've done it before so you can do it again. No matter what it is, I encourage you to stop for a moment to consider your why and lead yourself consciously into the infinite life that only you can create.

What insights did you have when you read this passage? What's something new that you'd like to try?

40. Sorting Your Thought Garbage

I noticed something the other day about how our household trash is separated. There are three bins, each with different pick-up days for organic waste, recycling, and garbage. What I remarked on was that when separated this way, there is so little actual garbage. In fact, in our neighborhood, garbage only needs to be picked up once every three weeks whereas the recycling and organic waste is picked up more frequently. It got me thinking. How much mental and emotional junk that we carry around with us could be sorted out like we do our day-to-day garbage?

Okay, so this one's gonna get a little messy.

As humans, we tend to rely on our inherent propensity to suffer. We're so good at it that often we don't even realize we are suffering until the load becomes too heavy to bear. And by the time it does come to the surface, and we try to get rid of it, the very weight of the garbage we've collected prevents us from being able to get to the end of the driveway to dispose of it. There's no better time than right now to start separating your thought garbage. I'm not talking about getting rid of it; I'm talking about taking a good look at it and making a conscious decision about what you want to do with it. Wouldn't it be amazing to discover that when organized this way, you had way less garbage than you thought you did?

We don't think twice about getting rid of things that are past their expiration date in the fridge. So why on earth do we hold onto so many old thoughts? Like expiration dates, we can take inventory of our mental fridge and remove any sour thoughts or rotten stories that don't nourish us. Good news is I have three thought bins for you so you can begin to sort your junk.

Expired Thoughts (Garbage)
These are literally old thoughts that you forgot you had. Thoughts that you've been holding onto way past their expiration date. These are potentially the most dangerous of all because, like food that's gone bad, they can fester and make you very sick.

Recycled Thoughts
These are thoughts that you can reframe and repurpose for your new paradigm. These may include old ways of thinking that are no longer serving you or limiting you in the present. Once you've sorted through these, you can repurpose them. This is all about transforming current negative thoughts about past behaviors into lessons that you can use as tools to help move you forward in the present.

Organic Thoughts
These are the thoughts that you notice are there and then let pass through without acting on them. This is where your response-ability lives, where you don't take things personally and can't be triggered into reacting defensively.

We've all become expert thought collectors, often without giving ourselves the time to consider the thought before we respond or just stuffing it down or pushing it way back on the shelf and forgetting about it. There's no better time than right now to start separating your mental and emotional garbage and making room for fresh new thoughts that will nourish you today.

Draw three thought bins, *Expired Thoughts*, *Recycled Thoughts*, and *Organic Thoughts*, and see what you learn about yourself when you sort your thought garbage!

41. The Journey Is the Thing

Twenty years ago, on the fourth floor of a steamy dance studio in New York City, I had just finished teaching my high-energy jazz class. I smiled at my sweat-drenched students as they shuffled out of the studio. They looked exhausted but content, having quite literally left it all on the dance floor. Some took the time to thank me for the class on their way out, while others rushed away to their next class, audition, or survival job.

I admired the way they cobbled together their days, which fluctuated and flowed between big dreams and huge disappointment. Cuts and callbacks, inspiration and perspiration. Their indefatigable stamina on the dance floor was matched only by their determination and passion for their art.

On this particular day, I noticed one student lingering behind as I packed up my things. I had known her for almost a year by then and saw her in class at least three times a week. She was one of my regulars, a truly dedicated student. Although twenty years have passed since we first met, I can vividly remember the very first time I saw her and our first encounter on the elevator ride up to the studio. Something about her compelled me to say hello to her in that moment, on that particular day. I asked her whose class she was taking, and she barely looked up from her well-rehearsed show-no-fear-act-cool-and-focus-on-her-feet stance to reply, "Hopkins." I smiled just as I am smiling right now because I knew that she had something very special, and I was grateful the universe had guided her to me.

But back to the story . . .

"What's up?" I asked her as she reached into her dance bag.

"I have something for you," she said, offering me a beautiful teacup and saucer she had made. Wrapped around the belly of the cup was a painted inscription that read: "The journey is the thing" with my name as the attribution.

"Did I say that?" I asked her.

"You always say that!" she laughed.

I was flattered that she had taken the time to make me something, but a little surprised that her biggest takeaway from the endless hours she had spent with me in the classroom were those five words: the journey is the thing.

Looking back now, I can see what high praise it was that she received the true essence of my teaching—maybe even before I knew what I was doing! I have indeed lived my life by that principle and endeavored to impart the message to my students that it is the journey which makes the dance sweet.

My student was just starting out in her professional career back then but in retrospect so was I! Although it may have appeared as if I was the established one, after all I was the teacher, the truth is, just like my students, I was cobbling together my existence, barely eking out a living. Unbeknownst to them, I was still on a student visa, barely making ends meet. I wasn't even allowed to audition for the shows I was preparing them for. Still, I never felt like an imposter. I felt completely at home teaching these brilliant artists. My lack of résumé credits at the time didn't hold me back, but rather allowed—even required—me to rely more deeply on who I was than what I had done.

Looking back, I now see that my student taught me a great lesson that day, even if I am only beginning to learn it in this moment. What I taught in the classroom was so much more than steps. It had nothing to do with what credits I had, how fabulous my combinations were, or the number of students that were in my class. It was about igniting the purpose and joy in whatever we do and understanding that whether you are going from a jeté to a pirouette or from a classroom to your day job, life can be danced every place you go because like the inscription said: "The journey is the thing."

The teacup my student gave me will always remind me our chance meeting on the elevator that day and the kismet that she had come to study with me. It is no surprise to me that she went on to have a marvelous career, and I as I sit here taking a sip from that very same cup, I feel grateful to have been part of her journey.

Where in your life might you be making an impact on someone else without even knowing it?

42. The Gifts in Grief

In his song "Seasons of Love," composer Jonathan Larson contemplated how to measure the value of one year in a human life, which, as the refrain goes, is 565,600 minutes. Today, I am contemplating the value of the lessons learned from lives lost and the paradox that there is a gift in grief, if we choose to receive it.

Spring 2018
I remember feeling Mom's presence all around me that day. I had just finished setting up the patio furniture for Dad. She welled up inside me as I sat where she should have been sitting on those first warm days of Spring. "Don't you just love it!" she'd blurt out, her knees pulled up to her chin as if to try and contain her excitement, childlike in her pleasure of the first warmth of spring.

The tulips had just started their annual pre-show, preparing for their short-run, five-star performance before they faded into the heat of summer. Her toes would curl up to balance her heels on the edge of the patio chair. Deformed and non-compliant, they'd stretched out in opposite directions with remnant chipped nail-polish from a glamorous event, her bone spurs protruding from endless hours of tap dancing. "Can you believe it?" she'd exclaim as if to pinch herself that this was her life. Expertly balanced in her tucked position on the chair, she'd reach out with one hand to pick up her glass of pinot grigio. She'd sip and then sigh, as if to marvel at her good fortune, feeling just a little bit embarrassed by it for a split second. Just as quickly, she'd brush it off with her signature bravado, perfectly playing the part of leading lady which she was to all of us, but especially to him.

Summer 2018
Almost four months later, I sat at my dining room table in Burlington. The summer felt long and full but somehow a bit empty too. It was hard to believe that I'd never be asked again to "come sit" or stay up too late together, drinking wine, laughing until we cried, sometimes saying things we wished we hadn't. She'd stare at me and sigh, "Ah, Lisa," which made me crazy because I thought somehow that she wasn't really listening. I know now that she heard more than I could imagine and that she *felt* me like only a mother can, listening for everything I wasn't saying, reading between the lines.

Fall 2018
Fall would never feel the same. If I could, I would call her to tell her about our new NYC apartment. I'd share some new music or a video of a step I made up. I imagine what fall might have been like for her if things

had worked out. I can visualize her leaving her house, dance bag slung over her shoulder as she walked into town to teach her tap class. Weird to think how close those women came to experiencing the immense joy she would have brought into their lives. I wonder if she'd take the time to stop and look at the canal as she crossed it or if she'd wait until she was on her way back, feeling energized from sharing what she loves with her students. Tiny and fierce, she'd strut across that bridge. She'd get there early to make sure everything was set up. No one would ever suspect that she was the least bit nervous, and the moment she put on her tap shoes, she was home.

I am eternally grateful to have shared this passion for dance with Mom. When we danced together, time slipped away, except for the rhythm we kept in our feet. The other day, I when put my tap shoes I thought about how it just doesn't feel the same without her. Sometimes tap dancing just makes me sad.

In November 2024, it'll be seven years since I lost my mother. 3,959,200 minutes. And though I miss her dearly, I know that she is all around me in everything I do, and I have a massive amount of gratitude for the gifts that have come from the grief.

As counterintuitive as it seems, I encourage you, if you've suffered loss of any kind, to look for the gifts, to look for the lessons, to look for the growth, to look for what has been shown to you through this passage in your life.

The Places Where There Are Spaces

I am grateful to have been shown that I am resilient and strong, even in the darkest of moments.

I am grateful to have grown a deeper relationship with my dad, far beyond what I might ever have imagined.

I am grateful to have known the absolute love of a mother, which remains now even more strongly than it did when she was mortal, and I feel her love inside me today and forever and a day.

Reflect on a time when grief led to unexpected growth. How did this transformation manifest in the form of a gift or new insight?

43. Lessons from the Lake

I stepped outside with my coffee as I do most mornings, no matter the season, and breathed in the crisp January air. The lake had frozen over and was covered with a vast white blanket of calm, glistening snow that stretched out and winked at me as its crystals caught the morning sun. It waited patiently for me as I cautiously stepped down onto its frozen surface, worried about the unlikely chance that I might fall through.

As I stood firmly with both feet on the lake, my apprehension transformed into a feeling of joy that wasn't there just moments earlier. I felt simultaneously like the participant and the observer, breathing in the fresh air as the lake, like a blank canvas, offered me an invitation to create. I brushed some snow away with my foot and was delighted to find that just under the snow was a pristine patch of smooth ice. I could see right through the ice to a rock that lay beneath and felt my heart start to race just a little bit as I put down my coffee and reached for the shovel and a broom. I felt inspired to create a skating rink.

Sometimes, I can see so many possibilities that I miss what's in front of me. Suddenly, my mind was flooded with ideas and visions of what I needed to do to make the rink and I was skating dangerously close to turning this serene moment into a project. I managed to slow down my racing thoughts by allowing the simple motion of the shoveling bring me back to the present, and as I concentrated on clearing the snow, I felt more and more at peace. Fresh creative thoughts started to drift and flow into my mind. I allowed them to pass through me without acting upon or assigning meaning to them and simply returned to the peaceful rhythm of the clearing. I was reminded of the monks who rake sand and remembered reading somewhere that the act of raking can help to bring order and peace to a wandering mind.

After I had shoveled the snow away, I took my broom and began to polish the ice with a back-and-forth motion that made the ice shine. I thought about my neighbor and the ice rink he had been engineering over the past few days, diligently flooding the lake trying to achieve the perfect surface for skating. There are many ways to paint a canvas and an infinite number of reasons for doing things that we do. It's what makes us unique artists of our own lives. I smiled at the irony that, at least for me that morning, the rink was already there.

The lake offered me a lesson that day about what lies beneath if we chose to look.

Reflect on the importance of paying attention to what's right in front of you and what you might be overlooking in your life.

44. Reconnecting Lost Signals

We've all experienced the frustration of losing our signal or worse yet being disconnected from the Wi-Fi. It's clear when it happens in a coffee shop, as all the guests look up from their devices for the first time in unison. Coffee shops used to be gathering places, for connection—human connection. Historically, cafés were where thinkers would gather, a place for lively debate and critical thinking. Many coffee houses became popular because of the famous poets and writers who frequented them. And you know what, it may be that coffee shops are still frequented by poets and writers, but we'll never know because no one ever talks to anybody. These days, the only conversations you hear are the brief exchanges between barista and customer communicating just enough to make sure the right size and flavor of coffee are ordered. And the only inquiry is about getting the Wi-Fi password before you sit down—hopefully close to a plug so you can stay charged.

Sad as it is, at least we know right away when we become disconnected from the internet. What would be different if we paid this much attention to when

The Places Where There Are Spaces

our internal connections and signals are lost? What if we were as interested in taking care of our personal operating systems and recharging our own drive? The signs of a disruption in digital service and an internal system disturbance aren't that different at first. You know that panicked feeling that we feel when we lose Wi-Fi? It isn't unlike the response we feel in our bodies when we feel off-centered in our internal systems. The reasons why we become disconnected require more understanding, or dare I say inquiry, than the on-off explanation of what happens when we go offline on our binary digital devices.

There's so much more than a password and a plug between what turns us on and what turns us off. But until we understand what our personal core processing unit consists of, we won't be able to learn what these signals mean. Maybe the disconnect has something to do with a value that is being challenged or an underlying fear or limiting belief that needs to be addressed. There is an opportunity here to consider the importance of noticing and listening to our internal signals. Drawing awareness around when we've gone offline with our values or purpose will help us remain connected to ourselves and stay plugged in to our unique frequency.

I still wish there were more coffee shops without Wi-Fi, so that we could convene and commune like the good old days. It's a wake-up call to how dependent we all are on the internet and how reliant we have become on external factors to motivate us. Although we might be physically in one place, more often than not, our minds are elsewhere. It's not natural. No wonder we are all stressed out and overwhelmed. And it has nothing to do with the coffee!

So next time you lose your hi-speed internet connection, slow down and reconnect with yourself. There are no quick fixes. No passwords or plug-ins. Just an opportunity to learn and discover what is important—to you.

Where in your life do you feel disconnected from yourself? Take a moment to journal about what's important to you and why.

45. The Magic of Letting Go

When I was a kid, I used to stand in the doorway of my bedroom and press my arms as hard as I could against the doorframe for thirty seconds and then step away to feel my arms magically rise up. How wondrous it was to feel that involuntary lightness. I never much cared to wonder why it happened but was completely delighted each time that it did!

Years later, when I was teaching dance in New York City, I discovered that a similar principle could be applied to increasing flexibility. One dancer would stand against the wall while the other helped them raise their leg up. When the dancer with the leg in the air had stretched as far as they could go, they were instructed to press down as hard as they could against their partner's hold to create resistance. The interesting part was when they stopped resisting and let go, their flexibility increased. They were able to stretch even further than they had before.

Today, through my lens as a coach, I can't help but wonder if this principle can be applied to the way we approach our lives. What things in life are we resisting that might be opportunities for growth

The Places Where There Are Spaces

if we consciously choose to let them go? Think about it. What would be different if we voluntarily stopped resisting things in our lives?

Resist means to fight against or oppose, to refuse to accept or be changed, or to stop oneself from doing something that one wants to do.

Do you know how much energy that requires?

Each of these definitions imply that there is something undesirable on the

other side, an adversarial person, thought, or thing that you are using all your might to keep out, not to mention exhausting yourself in the process. But what if you reframed resistance as a tool that increases your flexibility when used consciously, as my students did all those years ago in my dance class? What if resistance was an indicator of a place to grow, as opposed to a primitive defense mechanism that operates on fear? If you're a *Star Trek* fan, you'll recall the mantra of the enemy Borg: "Resistance is futile." But resistance is not futile at all!

If we draw awareness around where in our lives we are resisting, we can also shine light on how we can use resistance to stretch the limits of what's possible, to increase our edge. We do this not by continuing to resist but by letting go. Not because you can't resist any longer, but because it serves your growth.

What would be different if you voluntarily stopped resisting things in your life?

If you assert your will against the energy of an event that has already happened, it is like trying to stop the ripples caused by a leaf dropped into a still lake. Anything you do causes more disturbance not less. When you resist, the energy has no place to go.

—Michael A. Singer, *The Untethered Soul*

46. The Power of Energetic Choice

Susan was dragging her feet because her glorious and much-needed weekend away in the country was being cut short. It was time to get back to the city for a work event that she had committed to attend that evening. She told her colleague weeks ago she would attend and, even though she wasn't really feeling it, she mustered up the fortitude to pack away her cozy sweats and head back to the city to put on her cocktail attire.

I think we can all relate to how hard it can be sometimes to do things that we don't really feel like doing.

Let's face it, we don't live in a bubble and there will always be things demanding our attention that we wish were easier, more comfortable, alluring, or just plain fun to do. But for the things that we know we're going to do anyway even though it might feel out of our control, we always have a choice about *how* we are going to show up. It's what I call *Energetic Choice*.

Although Susan was able to muster enough energy to leave the countryside, the impetus came from the low-frequency energetic choice that I call *I have to*. There are times when it feels like soldiering on is the only choice we

The Places Where There Are Spaces

have, especially if it's expected of us or associated with the limiting beliefs of what success is "supposed" to look like. It's also why so many of us experience burnout.

Susan's mindset was fueled by obligation. Although *I have to* can catalyze a certain amount of energy toward a goal, it is an unsustainable energetic choice that can deplete our energy and engagement when we need it most, because it requires force, and force burns up a lot of energy. It can also trigger frustration, judgement, and anger, especially when things like traffic, a coffee stain on your shirt, or an urgent call from one of your children or colleagues inevitably comes up, threatening to impede your progress. It's no surprise that they say when it rains it pours!

When you are operating from *I have to*, your capacity to handle these kinds of obstacles is limited, because your energy is already being spent on soldiering through. With each thing that might interfere with Susan's push to show up (remember, *I have to* is characterized by force), it becomes easier to slip into resentment and overwhelm which are characteristics of the energetic choice I call *I can't*.

As Susan was getting ready that morning, she received a text from the event host who didn't ask so much as strongly suggest that she speak that night. (Keep in mind, she was already reluctantly pulling herself together as she transitioned from her country zone to her city self.) This triggered Susan into the energetic choice I call *I should*. Although a little higher frequency on the choice capacitor, *I should* is still a fear-based energetic choice fueled by shame. Your ability to do something isn't in question here; in fact, knowing you that could do it makes it even harder, especially when you don't really want to. When Susan's colleague suggested she speak that night, she felt guilty because although she knew she could do it, she didn't want to. It's often easier to identify what you don't want than what you do want.

Instead of caving in and saying yes because she thought she should, Susan told the colleague she would let them know. By giving herself the space to consider what she was *going* to do, she began to get clearer about what she *wanted* to do, which was to simply enjoy the event. She felt her stress ease and the pressure slip away as she shifted into the state of *I want to.*

When we want to do something, we feel more confident, energized, and connected to our reasons why we do things. Susan's initial reluctance to attend the event had transformed into feeling excited about connecting with her community. She was able to let go of feeling like she had no choice and felt grateful to be in a position where she got to decide.

Susan had arrived at *I get to*. It's the energetic choice that allows you to be in the moment with whatever you are facing and appreciate all that it offers. It's choice with gratitude. She called her colleague and told them she was looking forward to seeing them at the event. Then she thanked him for the opportunity to speak and respectfully declined.

Where in your life do you identify with being in any of these energetic choices? What would change if you shifted from *I can't* to *I get to*?

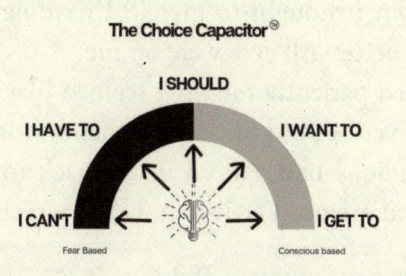

The Choice Capacitor®

I SHOULD

I HAVE TO   I WANT TO

I CAN'T   I GET TO

Fear Based   Conscious based

47. When Your Strength Becomes Your Weakness

It was thirty years ago on a sweltering summer day in New York City, up on the fourth floor of a steamy and non-air-conditioned dance studio, right smack in the middle of Times Square. All the pros took class there, alongside the aspiring dancers who dreamed of making it on the great white way. You couldn't even see out the windows that were completely steamed over and the energy in the room was palpable. I had just struck the final pose of the high-energy jazz combo having quite literally left my all on the dance floor when the teacher—who had trained some of the most famous dancers and later became my mentor—started walking slowly toward me. There was a kind of hush in the studio as my sweat-drenched classmates parted to let our teacher pass. I felt the beads of sweat running down my nose as I held the pose. *This was going to be my moment*, I thought to myself. I have never danced harder or better. All eyes were on me.

It waited patiently for what seemed like an eternity as he hobbled toward me, cane in hand, from the front of the studio. I had danced in the back row that day and every day since I arrived in NYC, which according to the unspoken pecking order was exactly where I belonged. The Broadway veterans held the first-row spots. When he finally reached me, he stopped and stood so close that I could smell his breath. "Hey, Canada," he said. I smiled to myself. Maybe he didn't know my name but at least he remembered I was the green kid from the Great White North! I still held the pose, ready to receive the compliment. But what happened next was not at all what I hoped for or expected. The two words that came out his mouth next rocked my world: "Too strong." That's all he said before he turned his back on me and walked away. I was devastated. I have never felt so deflated. What followed was a deli roast chicken, a case of beer, and a whole lot of tears. I had never felt so knocked down and certainly never been criticized for my strength. I prided myself on my bold, dynamic style. Back home in Canada, I was often complimented for my strength. It's what made me stand out. Ironically, it was also the very thing holding me back from growing as an artist. If I wanted to thrive in this industry, I had to learn the hard lesson that my strength was also my weakness.

Nowadays, in my coaching practice, I have found that it isn't uncommon for my clients to default to their strengths. They rely on doing things the same way because there is lots of evidence to support that it works, and so they assume that since it worked before, that it will always work. And I can't really blame them either, since most of these strengths and habits are behind their high levels of success. The thing is when we default to our strengths—to what we always do because it works, or because it's expected of us—we end up overshadowing aspects of ourselves and our potential to expand and develop in other areas. The danger here is that when we define ourselves by our strengths, we limit our possibilities. Take for instance an actor who is so well-known for their brilliant comedic work that they get passed over for any dramatic roles because they quite literally can't be taken seriously. Leading with what we you are known for has its advantages at first, if that is what is called for. It's a no-brainer to select you. You have become so competent in that area of your life that you don't even need to think about it. It's expected, and you know how to deliver. It feels familiar; therefore, it must be right. We all walk a fine line between getting into the groove and falling into a rut with any established routine or habit. But what are you missing out on by resorting to always doing things the same way?

Our strengths don't need to define us. They can be valued tools in our tool kit or jewels in our collection that we can consciously call upon them when we choose. They are well developed and polished, so have no fear—they won't be going anywhere. And when you aren't using them, I promise you that you will discover other new and interesting items on your menu of abilities. Let go of being the expert and adopt a beginner's mindset. Acknowledge your strengths but don't rely on them.

The Places Where There Are Spaces

Although it felt like my teacher was criticizing me when he told me I was too strong, I am forever in his debt for teaching me the invaluable lesson that my strength was where my weakness lay.

Where are you missing opportunities because you are defaulting to your strength?

48. Living Life as a Mosaic

There was a beautiful mosaic candle bowl that sat in the bay window of our kitchen when I was growing up. I was mesmerized by the way the tiny colored glass tiles glowed when the candle was lit. My mom knew how much I loved it, and when I moved out, she gave it to me. It has shone in every single place that I have lived since I left home that day. I light it, almost every evening, and when I do, Mom is home with me again, no matter where I go.

In some ways, my candle reflects how I lead my life—collecting pieces and experiences as I go, fitting them together to encompass all of who I am, forming a beautiful, colorful ever-evolving mosaic. Some pieces adhere and stay with me, others are let go. It's about synthesis for me. Soaking things in without trying to hold on to them, experiencing them as they pass through me. Some elements are absorbed and remain but are assembled in new ways. My life is the sum of many different and beautiful shards, some rich with color, some perfectly clear. Some smooth and polished, others sharp and rough. All these pieces contribute to who I am today, and I will continue to transform as I add new ones to my mosaic.

Apparently, the best way to create a mosaic is from the inside out, leaving space between the pieces for the grout which connects the pieces together. Perhaps life's "grout" is made up of our values and the lessons we've learned along the way—the things that hold us together.

I noticed that when a candle is new, my bowl doesn't glow very well. The most beautiful light is cast in the mosaic bowl when it burns low, closer to the wick, closer to the core.

Take a moment to recognize all the beautiful pieces that make up who you are. Shine the light on different parts of your candle. Embrace where you are right now, draw from what you have, and build from there. As you continue to piece it together, something new and beautiful will form from the little pieces you are collecting and those within you already. You always burn brightly to me, dear reader.

What are the values, experiences, and life lessons that make you uniquely you?

49. Mental Blocks

I had a mental block. And that mental block was literally a block. Let me explain!

For the first time in my life, I had been treating myself to a personal trainer once a week. From the start, it was important for me to let my trainer know that even though I might seem like I know what I'm doing, I have little to no experience in the weightlifting realm and I really wanted to be sure that my "smart" body wasn't making stupid choices about how to do things. She understood what I was saying and went on to share with me that, for her, the assumptions went the other way and that she often had to prove to her clients she knew what she was doing despite her slight physique and young age. She isn't much bigger than a flea and is barely twenty-two years old. She also happens to be an award-winning weightlifter.

I appreciated her candor and assured her that I could tell already that she knew her stuff, and she had nothing to prove to me. And so, our work together began with a foundation of honesty, mutual understanding, and respect, despite how easy it might have been to assume or make judgements based on our preconceived notions or appearances.

The Places Where There Are Spaces

She always keeps our workouts varied and interesting from battle ropes (never have I felt less elegant) to the sled, which entails channeling my inner quarterback.

On this day, she pulled out a small black block about sixteen inches high and started to demonstrate the next exercise. I watched as she easily jumped up and down off the block and an unfamiliar feeling came over me. It was fear. It was my turn and I stepped in front of the block, preparing to do the exercise. I stood there staring at it. I couldn't move. "C'mon you got this, Lisa! It's easy!" I heard my trainer saying. She seemed surprised by my hesitancy. I bent my knees, preparing to jump, but something in my brain stopped me.

Navigating fear is a big part of what I do in my work as a life coach, so I am very interested to understand what was going on with me that day at the gym. I truly believed what my mind was telling me, that I couldn't do it. It supported its reasoning by creating vivid storylines about what was sure to happen when I inevitably missed the box. Visualization is a powerful tool. Imagining that we are relaxing on a beach or achieving success can stimulate related emotional and physical responses (like heart rate decreasing or a feeling of confidence). Likewise, it can work against us, as it did for me in the gym that day, by envisioning what falling off the box would look and feel like.

My trainer lowered the height of the block, and I stepped up and jumped off (albeit reluctantly). I was even able to easily leap back up and land on one leg. Still, I was completely convinced that there was no way I could do it with two feet. "Just try it once," she kept saying. "I'll catch you if you fall." No amount of encouragement was working, so she downgraded me to a step. I managed go up and down a few times before I came to a standstill again, and I couldn't do that either. (When we try to overcome or resist our fears, the voice in our head gets louder.)

It's counterintuitive, but I wasn't angry with myself or ashamed because I couldn't do it; in fact, I found it curious and even a little bit funny. I knew instinctively that there was a lesson to be learned from this experience and despite what I initially thought, it wasn't about overcoming my fear. My focus transformed from conquering my fear to understanding it.

I thought it might be interesting to look at my story to see if there were any inner blocks that were holding me back that day.

There are four inner blocks that can hold us back or affect our ability to move forward with things we want to do. In coaching school, we used the acronym "GAIL" to remember them by.

G is for gremlin, your inner critic. The voice in your head that tells you you're not good enough. In my story, if the gremlin was responsible for holding me back, it might have said something like: *Don't do it, you'll just embarrass yourself* or *You're not strong enough*. But I wasn't hearing that message.

A is for assumption, the expectation or belief that because something has happened in the past, it will happen again. Now that's interesting because somewhere deep down there may have been a time when I hurt myself trying something similar and I believed that this might be what was holding me back. But I didn't think that was it.

I is for interpretation, a point of view, opinion or judgement that you create about an event, situation, person, or experience and believe to be true. I might have interpreted what happened as a weakness or waste of time but that wasn't the case at all. (Who knows what my trainer's interpretation was, but we're looking for my inner blocks not hers!)

L is for limiting belief, something that you've adopted and accept about life, yourself, your world, or the people in it that limits you in some way. So many things could fall under this heading in my story, including limiting beliefs about age, health, strength, or courage, but I didn't really feel any of those.

So, what was going on that day?

I have heard it said that everything you've ever wanted is sitting on the other side of fear. And, in some instances, that may be true. Fear can sometimes be a motivator, especially if you ascribe to the idea that overcoming it will bring you everything that you want. But you know what I'm realizing as I write this? I did have a limiting belief that day. The limiting belief was that I'm supposed to overcome my fear! The belief that when you are faced with something that scares you, you are supposed to push through it regardless.

I spent at least fifteen minutes more with my trainer, who tried her best to convince me to conquer the block, to no avail. The funny thing is that I thought I wanted to do it, but now in retrospect I realize that I couldn't have cared less! I am grateful that it happened though, and for the lesson. The block wasn't a mental block. It was just a block.

Think of a situation when one of these inner blocks was affecting your performance. What do you think would be different if you drew awareness around what was motivating or holding you back?

50. The Art of Perspective

I used to get so frustrated when people couldn't see things the way I saw them, especially the people I love the most. Not because I needed to be right, but because I wanted to share the beauty I see in the world. People would call me an optimist and say I always saw the glass half full, but that never sat right with me. The glass is neither empty nor full; it is simply a glass. For me, life is about what you put in the glass, and then whether you choose to drink it.

The other night after dinner, I happened upon one of those magical moments that only reveal themselves when you stop trying. Our adult daughter is back in our orbit again after a year abroad. And while we are overjoyed to have her near once more, a conscious recalibration of our new family rhythm is required, and it demands patience, space, and breath. It is not lost on me that this is a precious opportunity to be as in the moment as we can with each other and to refrain from filling in the very spaces we are trying to create with assumptions, interpretations, and well-intentioned quick fixes.

It was the first home-cooked meal we shared together in our new place since she had returned, and it was quite late when we decided to take an after dinner walk in the rain. It was dark as I walked slightly ahead of my daughter and husband on the dampened sidewalk, breathing in the fresh air and enjoying listening to them chat as they trailed behind me. The misty rain felt amazing on my face, and I smiled as they followed me in no particular direction. (Okay, full disclosure: remember when I said I wanted to share the beauty I see in the world with the people I love? I had seen a place on one of my solo walks that I wanted to show them. I didn't mention it because I had no idea if it would be open, or even if we'd get that far, but I would be lying if I didn't say I had a wee bit of an agenda.) In any case, they followed me, and I savored the moment, reminding myself that even if we never got there, it was already very special.

The parking lot was desolate when we arrived, and my heart sank a little because it didn't look open. But I thought I'd try the door anyway, and even though it looked like no one was there, it opened. I was delighted!

The soda plant did not disappoint. Twinkling lights were strung from the lofted ceilings of what once was a rundown soda bottling plant for Venetian Ginger Ale. Art displayed everywhere we looked, and even more magical when I had stumbled upon it earlier that week. The place looked like it had been transformed by fairies.

What followed was a masterclass in perspective. You can learn so much about a person by how they see things.

We wandered around the cavernous warehouse discovering art in every nook and cranny. Even the fire hoses and fuse boxes became art in our eyes. We learned about each other and ourselves that night as we laughed, considered, and shared our different points of view. It was refreshing to exchange thoughts and ideas freely, without argument or seeking agreement. There is no right or wrong when it comes to art, just an invitation to look.

There's an opportunity to apply this lesson to the interpretations that we are so quick to make in our day-to-day lives. Interpretations are one of the most common inner energy blocks that hold us back from experiencing a more fulfilled life. When we don't consider other points of view, we are restricting ourselves to seeing the world in just one way.

When we got home that night, I set an intention not to interpret the reasons why our daughter was home with us. The glass is neither half full nor half empty; it is simply a glass. And while she is here, I choose to drink her in and savor every single moment.

How has exposure to different viewpoints and interpretations enriched your understanding of the world around you? What would be different if you were able to simply experience things rather than try to assign meaning to them?

51. Little Impacts Everywhere

So many of us want to make an impact in the world, to spend our short time here on this planet doing something that is meaningful. Create a legacy. Be remembered for something. Make a difference. But so often, in our quest to leave our mark on the world, we cease to slow down long enough to lead a remarkable life, moving so quickly through our days that we leave no space or time to behold what is in front of us.

I am hardwired to make a capital I impact in the world, and I have a vision of what that might look like and what gifts and talents I might use to move in that direction. But it occurs to me that it's the little everyday impacts that really make a difference. Saying hello to a stranger, trying something new, engaging in all aspects of life—noticing.

Living a remarkable life is available to all of us in every moment of every day, no matter what we are trying to accomplish in our lifetime. According to Merriam-Webster, the word "remarkable" is defined as "worthy of being or likely to be noticed." Noticing quite literally means "to see or become conscious of something or someone." And it is in that awareness

The Places Where There Are Spaces

that we have a chance to make little impacts everywhere along the way.

I like to call it compound interest: the more interest you take in others, the more value you bring to your own life and others and the legacy you are so eagerly trying to build. And it's so simple. Smiling at someone as you pass by or saying hello to a stranger can change the trajectory of their lives forever. And most of the time we won't even know we've done it. Do you have any idea of how much living-legacy potential there is in those lost moments because of our failure to exist in the here and now?

Noticing something new in your day-to-day life, seeing something you've seen before through new eyes, or considering a different point of view are all ways to consciously engage in our world. Sometimes, just slowing down long enough to take that interest in what someone is doing can make all the difference. There is little impact to be made everywhere.

It's easy to get swept up by passion or consumed by a cause or to spend your days searching for your purpose. Each and every one of us has the opportunity to spend our short time here on this planet doing something that is meaningful. Create a legacy. Be remembered for something. Make a difference. Every day. So go out, my friends, and live a remarkable life, in every moment. Surprise yourself. Notice and engage. Don't save it for tomorrow; invest in today. Compound your interest, pay attention, and embrace what's here right now.

What is one small thing you might do today that may create a lasting impact on others?

52. My Night at The Museum

I had no idea when the door slammed shut behind me out that my evening would be so enchanting. It was late spring on the Upper East Side, around 7 o'clock. After nearly three days of rain and gloom, the sun was peeking out just in time to set. I leapt at the opportunity to cure my cabin fever, threw a jacket over my at-home-only sweats and set off to catch the sunset over the reservoir. I felt instantly better as I stepped outside.

It was warmer out than I had anticipated, and I was definitely overdressed. I considered climbing back up the five flights of stairs to our apartment to change my clothes, but instead, I removed my jacket and tied it around my waist. I was looking shabbier by the minute but who was going to see me? There was no way I was going to miss the sunset.

It felt great to breathe the air and get my heart pumping on the two-mile walk around the reservoir. I reminisced about how quickly the spring semester had flown by and, since we'd be leaving the neighborhood in a few days, I decided to extend my walk down Museum Mile to take a few parting snapshots.

I sat on the steps of the magnificent Metropolitan Museum of Art and reveled in its grandeur. A musician, like a court jester, mamboed on the terrace as he switched from alto sax to clarinet, entertaining the passersby. It was idyllic. I couldn't have asked for more. In that moment, I felt like an image in a street artist's painting that might be called *The Met at Dusk*. I loved being part of the street scene and yet almost invisible, perfectly anonymous, with no expectations of myself or anybody else.

Just then, two young men passed by me, and I overheard one of them asking the other if he'd ever been to the Met. I turned and watched them go in. Before I could think, I found myself following them up the steps to the entrance. I asked the security guard when the museum closed, and he said they were open for another thirty minutes. I crossed the marble floor to the ticket booth and asked the woman behind the desk if they were still letting people in and what the price was for half an hour. I half expected her to tell me it was too late, but she smiled and told me that all I needed was a penny. *A penny? That's amazing*, I thought. The minimum suggested donation was a just a penny. I love New York.

Then I remembered running out of the house to catch the sunset. No wallet, just keys and my phone. She waited patiently as I desperately searched my pockets. I had never wanted a penny more. It was like the golden ticket to the magical kingdom. I must have been quite the sight in my baggy sweats and muddy work boots, jacket tied around my waist. Just as I was about to give up, I found a dime. Triumph! I presented it to her, holding her to her word. My defenses were up, armed and ready to be met with a discriminatory glance or some excuse that it was too late now to enter the museum. Instead, I was met with a gracious smile as the attendant accepted my dime and passed me through.

The Met is monumentally impressive in size. A half hour could barely get you through the Great Hall. Determined, I asked the security guard for his recommendation, and he suggested I check out the fashion exhibit downstairs. I followed his directions and found the exhibit which, although lovely (and on any other day of great interest to a thespian such as myself), wasn't what I was looking for.

It was then that I stumbled upon the American Wing, which I later discovered is the Charles Engelhard Court. Standing alone, surrounded by the most beautifully stoic and graceful bronzes and sculptures in the glass-ceilinged courtyard atrium, was one of the most profound "now" moments I've ever experienced. Never have I felt so mortal, these godlike figures looming over me, non-judgemental and surreal. I proceeded to wander through the living rooms of Tiffany and Frank Lloyd Wright, imagining what it must have felt like to live back then. I could have meandered for hours but knew it was time to go. On my way out, I stopped to look at a piece of ancient mosaic wall that dated back more than five thousand years. *That's two hundred generations*, I thought, moved by the notion that I was experiencing something that was created so very long ago. It was a reminder of how short our time is on this planet. I recalled the words of Albert Pike: "What we have done for ourselves alone dies with us; what we have done for others and the world remains and is immortal." It was profound to imagine who created that ancient mosaic wall, almost a sacred experience to be witnessing it for the first time.

I thanked the security guard as I exited the museum, and he nodded then locked the door behind me. An air of lightness came over me as I walked down the grand steps, now empty. I promised to return when I have more time but knew that no planned visit could ever compare to the experience I had that night—my night at the museum.

PS: I'm not sure if I imagined it, but walking home that night, out of nowhere and for no particular reason (as it wasn't a holiday), there were fireworks over the reservoir.

Reflect on a time when unexpected circumstances led to a magical experience.

53. The Paradox of Change

There's never been a time when I haven't felt like summer went by too quickly. Those longer summer days invited us to slow down and take our time, to play more and enjoy time with people we love. There's a melancholy that creeps in with a change of seasons I'm learning though that you can't long for something if you didn't experience something wonderful enough to be missed in the first place. I think nostalgic is a better way to describe how the transition to fall feels to me.

Whether it's the change of seasons, or a transition in your life, there's a paradox that comes with change that can be off centering. When we know things are going to be different, it can be scary. The only way we know that something is different is by comparing it to something else. If we are unsure what that "something else" will bring, it makes us long for or cling to what we once had. We can make more sense of this dichotomy once we recognize that two things can be true at the same time. It's not uncommon to feel simultaneously happy and sad, excited and trepidatious, nostalgic and pragmatic about the prospect of change. Change is

The Places Where There Are Spaces

inevitable but, as Buddha is reported to have said, suffering is optional.

There is a quintessential beauty to the fall season as the leaves magically turn color, offering astounding views of the glorious nature of Mother Earth. The vibrant colors are matched only by the deep blue melancholy that accompanies the crisp air, as the idle kayak knocks against the dock. But isn't that also wonderfully poetic in its loneliness?

I could choose to live in scarcity and mourn the loss of summer, or I can smile when I recall the early morning summer sounds of laughing ducks and seagulls singing high in the sky as they dive for fish. I could drown myself in worry about when I'll see my family next, or I can feel my heart warm when I remember hosting the family gathering at the lake for the last weekend of summer.

These memories are not being replaced now by the change of season. These memories are ours to keep and to take with us.

Soon, the skies will be ringing with the honking return of the Canada geese who, like bullies on the playground, take over the lake until the last vestige of open water freezes over and they finally migrate to warmer places for the winter. By then, we will be looking forward to the holiday season and creating new memories. Who knows, maybe if we put our minds to it, we might even take the time to live in each moment and enjoy the change that each new season brings.

Reflect on a significant change in your life and how it made you feel. Consider how change can evoke a mix of emotions.

54. Life Is a Wide-Open Stage

You'd be hard-pressed to find someone as passionate and stoic as the committed actor. I speak from experience, as I have had the honor of working with actors in one capacity or another my entire career. I am repeatedly astounded by their unwavering courage and integrity, often in the face of incredible vulnerability and all in service of the story. Actors are some of the most brilliant and gifted people in the world. They have this mystical, ineffable ability to transform themselves into the characters they play. They delve deeply below the surface to understand the needs and wants of their characters and what drives their thoughts, words, and actions. They seek to clarify intentions and motivate actions in alignment with the character's values and beliefs, so that they can operate from their character's' "why."

There's a lot we can learn from the actor's process and, for those of you who *are* actors, there is much that you can apply and benefit from in your own artistic methodology as you create your own life story.

William Shakespeare famously wrote: "All the world's a stage," and, as the bard so aptly observed, we are indeed all players on life's great world stage. Like actors, we spend our days in service of the story; however, our stories often revolve around what we think we are supposed to be rather than who we truly are. Many of us play multiple parts in our own lives, cast by a panel of limiting beliefs that dictate and determine what the role requires. We memorize and deliver the lines on cue, playing roles as written and directed by someone else. We are telling someone else's story, barely scratching the surface of who we really are, let alone diving deep into our motivation. It's easier to play a part that's already written and default to being a certain way than to develop a deeply committed self. Like a recurring role in a program on Netflix, it becomes expected of us to show up the way we always do in the many roles that we play in our lives.

Life is like a wide, open stage, just waiting to be set. Unlike theater, however, your story is real, and the story that you tell and the roles that you play are yours to create. Each of us is the lead in our limited-run production, but have you considered that we can also be the director? The role of director requires having a vision, making tough decisions, collaborating and, above all, leading.

We will appear in a multitude of scenes and roles in different stages throughout our life, leading toward the grand finale, which is the same for all of us. In theater, if you don't stand in your light, you won't be seen. Why should life be any different?

What stories are you telling yourself that could use a rewrite? Are there different roles in your life story that have yet to be created?

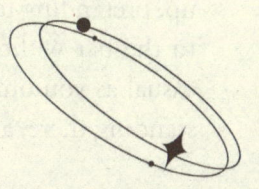

55. When Your Networking Is Not Working

You're at a networking event but haven't spoken to anyone yet. The room is crowded with a charged energy of what looks like everybody else connecting. You feel simultaneously invisible and painfully exposed in your discomfort, wondering how everyone else makes it look so easy. *I'll never be any good at this,* you think to yourself, feeling your hands go icy as your body temperature rises. *Is it getting hot in here?* You try to convince yourself that networking is good for you, that if you want to get ahead in your career, it's what you must do.

So, you push through the crippling fear, put on your game face, and begin scanning the room. You spot someone standing alone at the bar. They look nice enough, so you muster up the courage to begin the approach. *Why do the carpets at these events always look the same?* you wonder, as you move toward the bar. Catching yourself with your head down, you straighten up, pretending to be confident. You manage to make it to the bar without bolting for the exit and try to act casual as you order yourself a drink. Your target is still standing there, and while you wait for the bartender to pour your drink, you bravely glance over as nonchalantly as possible. They happen to look back at you and eye contact is made.

Don't look down, you say to yourself, your thoughts racing almost as fast as your pulse. Like a mantra, you start to recite the five C's of good eye contact: connection, concentration, conversation, confidence, and credibility. You repeat the list three times, each repetition reinforcing your determination to maintain strong eye contact. Then you remember reading somewhere that if you hold eye contact for more than five seconds, it can be misconstrued either as a signal that you are attracted to the person, or that you want attack them! So, you stop staring immediately and force an awkward hello. Despite what you might have feared, you do not perish in that moment. *That wasn't so bad*, you think, then you notice that they are returning the smile and saying hello.

There is an awkward silence that, like a chasm between you, threatens to swallow you up. Thankfully, the moment is interrupted by the bartender, who hands you your drink. You take a gulp and realize that it's your turn to say something before the window of opportunity to connect slams in your face.

Before you know it, you are spitting out some small talk about the weather, the wine, or the food, with just one goal now: trying to keep the conversation going. Anything is better than the shame of being the only one not talking to someone in the crowded room where everyone else is networking—isn't it?

The ice has been broken and you're both feeling a little more relaxed now, so you introduce yourselves. Your head tells you this is a good sign but you your body can feel the stakes getting higher and the pressure mounting as they ask the inevitable flow stopping question: "What do you do?"

You're caught off guard, suddenly defensive. Expectations rush in and your memory rushes out. You are positively stymied by the question. *What's the matter with me?* you wonder, making it even harder to think clearly. You can barely recall anything you've done, let alone qualify it. You vaguely remember creating an elevator pitch, but who the heck ever actually pitches on an elevator? The 5 C's are mocking you now like bullies in the playground. You look down.

Sound familiar?

Listen, networking is hard. And when it's not working, it's even harder. We've all been there. But we have far more choice in how to approach networking beyond forcing ourselves to do it because we think we should.

I always say to my clients that there is a distinction between decision and choice that is a real game changer in how we show up in the world energetically, in everything we do. Think of a decision as something that you've already made. It's typical black-and-white thinking. In this case, go or don't go to the networking event. Somewhere along the way, for whatever reason, a decision has been made and you are there at the event. The choice piece comes in with *how* you show up at the event or anywhere that you've already decided to go. That is where the alchemy and power of energetic choice lies.

When we feel that we have no choice but to push through or do something because it's good for us, or because we are afraid of what will be if we don't, then we are operating from fear-based thinking, and our power to show up to our true capacity is hugely diminished. The goal becomes simply to survive the ordeal.

Have you ever felt completely depleted and drained after one of those networking events? Well, it's no surprise! Operating in survival mode is unsustainable, not to mention completely counterproductive when it comes to networking! Your access to your full capacity to engage is limited because all your focus is on protecting yourself instead of promoting yourself!

Remember in our story when you couldn't find the words to answer the question: What do you do? That's your freeze response. You lost all access to your unique, brilliant energy because the fear of saying the wrong thing consumed you. And for those of us who find that our networking is not working, this is precisely why.

I have a couple of C's of my own to help you shift your energy and answer that inevitable "What do you do?" question. And these C words work in concert (I couldn't resist): curation and curiosity.

Unless we want to be defined by, and confined to, the limitations of what others know (or think they know), we want to curate our answer so that it invites curiosity. A curator's role is literally to select and care for what is shown or presented. In this case, your collection is composed of values that you hold and express in the world, and the value that you offer to those you work with. If we answer their question with a title or role that they will have heard of (think: composer, lawyer, actor, doctor, coach), then we are limiting any chance of making a unique impression and helping them file us away into any preconceived notions they have about those occupations instead. Face it, there are a million others out there doing what you do, but there is only one of you doing it the way you do it. That is where the true answer to the question lies.

I struggle with this question sometimes too, because when people ask me what I do, I could go in so many different directions. We all wear many hats in our multifaceted lives and, while that can be an absolute superpower, choosing one can put us in a box and listing them all can be overwhelming and confusing. So, I started to curate an answer that encompasses the essence of all that I do and the unique value that I bring. For instance, some of the roles I play in my life are teacher, writer, dancer, coach, podcast host. Here's a few curated answers bespoke to me:

> "I create safe spaces for creative self-expression and exploration."

> "I help people find artistry in all aspects of their lives."

> "I lead with a generous energy that helps elevate and inspire whoever I engage with."

The Places Where There Are Spaces

So, when I answer that dreaded question with one of these, I am tapped into my purpose and inviting curiosity. Inevitably, the next question that arises is: "How do you do that?"

I encourage you to try this exercise and bet that if you look more closely at what you do and all the roles you play in your life, you'll discover there is a through line, something that all of them share. Only you know what makes you truly unique and taking the time to curate your response will make answering the question easy because it comes from inside you, your essence.

I remember feeling the rush of counting all the business cards I had amassed when I was networking on the conference room floor all those years ago. I truly believed there was a correlation between the number of people I talked to and what determined a successful conference. I realize now that networking is about connecting not collecting and that connection is not just with who you are speaking too, but with yourself.

Create a sentence that encompasses the essence of all that you do and the unique value that you bring.

56. When Is Enough, Enough?

What does the word "enough" mean to you in this moment? Is it a kind of settling—*This is good enough for now*—or does it feel like gratitude: *We've got more than enough*. Maybe it's wrapped up in greed or scarcity, an insatiable hunger for more—*I don't have enough*—or perhaps it's a much-needed boundary, a primitive inner voice that rises up from inside and screams: *Enough is enough!*

It's safe to say we have all at one time or another reached a boiling point and finally found the strength to draw the line and stand by our non-negotiables. But what non-negotiables do we have for how we treat ourselves?

Why do we set the bar so high for how we show up for others but keep it so low for how we show up for ourselves? Used one way, enough can be empowering, a kind of catharsis as we finally stand in our truth. And yet the very same word, when turned on ourselves, has an astonishing self-destructive capacity: *I'll never be enough*. It's an overwhelming sense that we aren't rising to the expectations of others; therefore, we must be flawed or deficient.

But what does enough even mean? Is it defined by some sort of unreachable destination or perfect ideal that seems to get further away the closer we get? Our society places such a high value on fame, money, success, and beauty but if we don't take a moment to understand what our own values are, how can we begin to appreciate ourselves?

In her book *Emotional Agility*, author Susan David tells us: "Let go of unrealistic dead people's goals by accepting that being alive means sometimes getting hurt, failing, being stressed and making mistakes. Free yourself from ideas of perfection so you can enjoy the process of loving and living."

Enough said.

What non-negotiables do you have when it comes to yourself?

57. The Hurdles We Face in the Human Race

As if life as we know it isn't already disorienting enough, the recent Olympic games were called Olympic Games Tokyo 2020. One hundred years from now, our ancestors are going to have a difficult time understanding the chronology of this decade. It makes it look somehow like we *gained* a year—another lap around the sun—which is ironic when 2020 was a year when so many of us *lost* so much. But in the spirit of looking at things from different perspectives, let's remind ourselves that without experiencing loss, we can't experience it's opposite.

I looked up the antonym for the word "loss" and first entry that came up was not win or gain but recovery and finding.

You see, without loss, we can't know it's inverse. Acknowledging what we've lost sheds light on what we considered valuable in the first place. It offers us the opportunity not only to *re-cover* but to *un-cover* what has been hidden underneath and *dis-cover* gifts that we might not otherwise have found.

We've all had to ponder what is truly important to us and what values have given us the strength to

The Places Where There Are Spaces

soldier on despite the hurdles we've faced. In the end, it isn't about winning the race or how many hurdles we knock down along the way; it's about celebrating our small victories and the gifts of the journey itself—if we choose to recognize them.

We are all Olympians in the human race, which has only one finish line. How we get there is up to us.

Reflecting on the hurdles you've faced in life, what are some small victories and valuable discoveries you've made along the way?

58. Holiday Hangovers

As joyful as the holiday season always presumes to be, the limiting beliefs of how things are *supposed* to be are so ingrained in us that we practically set ourselves up for failure before we even begin. We place such high expectations on ourselves and others this time of year that if we aren't feeling festive "on cue" for whatever reason, we feel cheated, as if we're missing out on the joy that everybody else seems to be engaging in. It's pretty much a sink-or-swim, win-or-lose affair, complete with regrets of things you wished you had or hadn't said, a countdown to the inevitable holiday hangover.

It was nearing the holiday season, and after a perfectly lovely hike in the snow, I was inexplicably overcome by the kind of feeling that can be best described as malaise. I just love it when a word perfectly fits the feeling. The fact that it's a French word, and I was in La Belle Province, makes it even more of a *bon mot*. The *Oxford English Dictionary* defines malaise as "a general feeling of discomfort, illness, or uneasiness, whose exact cause is difficult to identify." It arrived unannounced, and without notice or provocation, and instead of just noticing it was there, and contrary to everything I know as a coach, I acted upon it. I lashed out at my husband. I was negative, confrontational, and just plain ugly, which, as defined by the *Oxford English Dictionary*, means "unpleasant or repulsive, especially in appearance," is an apt description of my behavior that day.

My husband has no problem *not* thinking about holiday preparations until the last minute, whereas I find myself trying to perfect everything ahead of time. Maybe it's my theater background. I just love staging and take pride in creating spaces for others to experience, to host produce and direct. Our different approaches to holiday preparation have the potential to create tension between us when I'm in the mood and he is not, like when he's busy with non-festive activities and I would rather him help me string the lights outside. And to be honest, the irony is it's not actually his help I'm after. I'm perfectly capable of doing it myself! It's my expectations of what decking the halls is supposed to look like, all wrapped up and delivered courtesy of the media.

Making things worse, when I'm stressed, I'm not tapped into knowing what I truly want or need, let alone communicating it to others. I sometimes fall into the trap of disguising my expectations by hinting and dropping clues, testing my loved ones and setting them up for failure. All to the tune of "It's the Most Wonderful Time of the Year."

As each calendar year comes to an end, it's easy to become hijacked by the fear of time running out. In our quest to show up joyfully with all the fixings, holidays

The Places Where There Are Spaces

can become hotboxes for expectations, exhaustion, and overwhelm. Our inner critics and self-saboteurs crank up the volume in our heads like a song on repeat, replaying all the things we said we would do, reminding us of what we haven't done.

All those expectations you hold for yourself, for the season, and for those you love are normal. But just because they're normal, doesn't mean they are required.

Remember that snowy day when I was wrapped up in my malaise and I lashed out at my husband because he wasn't helping me decorate? When I took a moment to stop and breathe, my malaise began to transform into its antithesis. Do you know what the opposite of malaise is? Comfort and well-being. When I allowed myself enough space simply to stop for a moment and breathe, it transported me back to the present to reconnect with gratitude for what truly is. All my expectations fell away because I realized that I already had everything I needed in that moment. I realized how incredibly grateful I was for my husband, and to be able to celebrate with loved ones. I also came to appreciate that if I didn't string another row of lights or hang another wreath, I am already enough. I have everything I need for a joyous holiday season. The only light needed is the light that shines inside of me. And I wanted to remind you the same: to give yourself the gift of living in the moment and allow yourself access to connecting to all the joy that you have inside you already. And, when those expectations threaten to take you down, remember that you are enough.

Make a list of all the reasons why you are grateful for yourself.

59. The Places Where There Are Spaces

There is infinite beauty to behold in the unplanned, unspecific moments that make up our lives. Rarely recognized or deliberate, they just happen. They are nowhere to be found on our copious lists or calendars, and yet they are everywhere, in each moment and in-between each of those moments, in everything we do.

They exist both in the extraordinary and, sometimes especially, in the seemingly mundane. Unattached to outcomes or goals, these moments are abundant in their capacity to evoke and delight, and yet are scarcely known—often overlooked—in our race to "live" our lives.

They linger and loiter just beneath the surface, gently simmering. Available to us in good times and bad, they stand by with an open invitation, ripe with possibility for a new storyline or a plot twist, ready to be created. They show up when you are least expecting them and unfold and transform only when you stop long enough to notice them.

It's where the muses and the fairies reside, and time seems to stand still—in the places where there are spaces.

Thirty spokes share the wheel's hub; It is the center hole that makes it useful. Shape clay into a vessel; It is the space within that makes it useful. Cut doors and windows for a room; It is the holes which make it useful. Therefore, profit comes from what is there; Usefulness from what is not there.

—Lao Tzu, *Tao Te Ching*

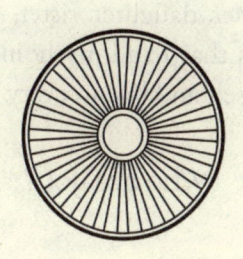

I Am

I have lived and worked alongside inspiring creative people my whole life. I know what it means to lead with passion and to follow my heart and what it feels like to perform at my highest level and—sometimes quite literally—leave it all on the dance floor. I strive to consort with my muse, who sings louder than the voices in my head that try in vain to hold me back from dancing to the music that I know is this beautiful life. I refuse to be defined by what I've done or make choices based on what I think I should be doing next. I am a proud mother, daughter, sister, and a wife. There are two countries that I call my home, but I aspire to find home in myself and live in every moment—wherever I am.

Who are you?

Gratitude

Three days after Broadway shut down in March 2020, we left NYC to isolate in Quebec. I am eternally grateful to my father for letting us stay, by ourselves, at his beloved Tir Na Nog. The magical chalet was named by my mother, after the Celtic tale of a place of eternal love and joy, where everyone lives forever, and nobody ever gets sick. They remain three of the most enchanted and creative months of my life.

During that time, despite my inclination to silo my vocations, I could no longer keep my two careers at arm's length. In fact, extending my reach was what I was being called to do–to connect with and hold space for my creative community, in my new capacity as a coach.

Later that Spring, I released my podcast *STOPTIME: Live in the Moment.* I had absolutely no idea how to do a podcast, only that I wanted to help. My first three guests were my students. Brilliant artists at the beginning of their careers all twenty years old, in Broadway shows that had been put on hold or canceled. I reached out to them and asked them if they wanted to have a conversation—they all said yes. To them I am grateful.

As the pandemic continued to draw on, it created a space for me to draw out reflections of my own that became solo episodes on my podcast. The response from listeners moved me profoundly and became the seeds of this book. If it weren't for my daughter Haley's encouragement, I may not have been brave enough to go solo. I am so very grateful to her for believing in me.

My mother-in-law Anna became one of my avid listeners and often took the time to respond to my musings. She also helped me with the first draft edit of this book. I am grateful to her for her support and for the even deeper connection we have forged through sharing my work.

To my lifelong pal Diane, who has known me forever and reminds me that I've been a writer all along.

To the love of my life and fellow dreamer. "Mon amour, my friend." I am forever grateful to have you by my side.

The Places Where There Are Spaces

There are so many wonderful writers out there with important and insightful things to say. I read them every morning while I drink my coffee. Without the inspiration of their words, I might not have felt as compelled to share my own. Here's just a few that have challenged my thinking, inspired, and delighted me:

Michael A. Singer
Sarah Lewis
Thich Nhat Hanh
Pema Chödrön
Elizabeth Gilbert
Adam Grant
Susan David
Don Miguel Ruiz
Kahlil Gibran

If you are interested in learning more about me reach out:

www.wideopenstages.com

Scan the code below to find links to my website and the STOPTIME:Live in the Moment Podcast

Printed in Canada